Selected Stories by Xuemo

Xuemo

Translated by Nicky Harman

中国大百科全书出版社
Encyclopedia of China Publishing House

First Edition 2018

ISBN 978-7-5202-0278-7

Copyright © 2018 by Xuemo

Published by Encyclopedia of China Publishing House

Fuchengmen Beidajie No.17, Xicheng District , Beijing, China

Tel:(86)10-88390739

http://www.ecph.com.cn

E-mail:limoyun2008@sina.com

Printed by October Printing Ltd., Company

Contents

Old Man Xinjiang

Old Man Xinjiang began to pack up his stall. It was still early. The sun, a dull yellowish-white lump of curd, had only just begun to move into the west. A breeze stirred the ochre earth and made the dead leaves rustle, bringing with it the smell of autumn. Old Man Xinjiang packed his fruit away, then started on the eggs. His stall was nothing more than two baskets and two pieces of cardboard. The eggs were piled on one of these, the other held the pears, each one of them soft to the touch, thin-skinned and-when you bit into them-running with a sweet cold juice which was good for coughs. Eggs and pears…that was all he had, simple to lay out and equally simple to pack away. He bought the fruit by the pound, paying 40 cents and selling them for 45; the eggs he bought for 20 cents each, selling them at 22 cents apiece. He could scrape a living from it, no more than that.

Old Man Xinjiang hoisted the carrying pole with a basket at each end onto his shoulder and headed off towards the east end of the village. He was a tall, thin man and he cast a long shadow which seemed to crawl beside him like a giant millipede. He scuffled quickly along, his eyes shining bright. The villagers watched him. 'Where are you going, old man?' someone asked. 'To hers,' he answered. They didn't ask who 'she' was. 'To give her money?' A grunt of assent. 'And you'll get your leg over in return, will you?' The others laughed. Embarrassed, Old Man Xinjiang tried to leave but he was surrounded. 'You're still up to it, aren't you?' Old Man Xinjiang lowered his baskets to the ground and thumped his aching back. 'Don't talk nonsense. I'm an old man.' There was a burst of laughter. 'You're never too old if you put your mind to it,' said one. And another added: 'If the tool's bust, what's wrong with a hand job? A bit of rubbing should do you nicely!' That was too much for Old Man Xinjiang; he shouldered the pole again and made off as fast as he could, hopping along like a rabbit.

'Hers' was a dilapidated shack with bits of plaster flaking off the back wall like diseased skin. When he arrived, the woman was busy filling in a ditch, her clothes and face covered in dust. She put down the wooden spade and slapped the dust away. They greeted each other briefly. The old man went inside. The paper window coverings let in little light and it was very dim. There was a *kang* bed, heated by a flue from the cooker. An old man with reddened eyes sat there, a pipe in his hand. He lit a touchpaper from the oil lamp, stuck it in the pipe bowl and breathed in till it flamed and smoke came out of his nostrils. He shifted when he saw Old Man Xinjiang and grunted a greeting. Old Man Xinjiang took a low stool and hunkered down, sitting very still.

'It's been another bad harvest this year,' said old Red-Eyes.

'Very bad,' agreed Old Man Xinjiang.

'What'll next year be like?'

'Who knows?'

'That's life, eh?'

The woman came in, slapping the dust from her clothes.

'Are you cold?' she asked, looking at him.

'Not really.'

'You should be wearing your winter jacket.'

'Yes, I should.'

'And your bedding needs a wash.'

'It does.'

'I'll dig those vegetables tomorrow, then I'll wash it for you the day after.'

'I'll do the vegetables,' said old Red-Eyes. 'You wash his

bedding. You can't tell what the weather's going to do.'

'Stay and eat with us,' said the woman. 'I'm going to cook noodles.'

But Old Man Xinjiang said: 'No, I won't stay. I'm off to the doctor's for a jab. I've caught a chill.'

'You should be wearing your winter jacket.'

'I should,' agreed Old Man Xinjiang. Picking up his carrying pole, he left. The old couple did not bother coming to the door.

Outside in the chill wind, his nose began to itch and he sneezed. He had the odd feeling there was a bug in his nostrils trying to squirm its way out. He needed that jab, he thought, wiping his nose. But it was just a cold-he couldn't complain, he hadn't been ill this year. He gave another loud sneeze.

There was hardly anyone at the doctors, just two men and a child. He picked out one of the pears, gave it to the child, and sat down. He waited for the men to say something but they sat silent, watching the child eating the pear and slurping dribble and juice. He wouldn't give away his pears to them, he thought, that wouldn't do at all. But the men helped themselves from his basket anyway, first one, then the other.

'Help yourselves!' Old Man Xinjiang said, 'Ripe pears are good for fever!'

When it was his turn, he said to the doctor: 'I want a jab. Give me penicillin, will you? That's the only one I know.'

The doctor smirked. 'You should be resting when you've got a cold. No more running after women or you'll exhaust your *yang-qi* and that'll be the end of you!'

Old Man Xinjiang went red. 'What nonsense! You're an educated man, Doctor, not a pig-ignorant villager...'

'Is it true you haven't been getting any?' asked the doctor, composing himself.

'How could I? When a woman's married to someone else, it's wrong!' Old Man Xinjiang felt a bead of sweat at the end of his nose. 'What counts in this life is loyalty to your friends.'

The doctor looked at him as he felt his pulse: 'But she was your wife first. There'd be nothing wrong with sleeping with her.'

'She...she...' Old Man Xinjiang stuttered, turning pale in his agitation.

'How old were you when the press-gang got you?'

'Twenty.'

'Was it really the morning after your wedding night?'

'Uh-huh.'

'And you really made it all the way back from Xinjiang on foot? You didn't get a ride?'

'Uh-huh.'

Old Man Xinjiang did not feel inclined to say anything more. He'd been asked the same questions hundreds of times, by this person and that, he was fed up with it. Yes, he was twenty, or perhaps a bit more. It was all so long ago that his memories had gone hazy, like a dream. What he did remember was that Xinjiang was very far away, and he'd been forced to go. There had been so many of them, they hadn't even roped them together. Press-gangs really did come and drag you out of your bridal chamber and take you to the army camp. He'd been on the march for years...When people asked 'What's Xinjiang like, then?' he just said: 'I don't know. All I thought about was my wife.' He hadn't even had time to see her face properly, but she was still his wife. So he deserted. The first few times, he'd been caught and flogged half to death. At the fifth attempt, he'd made it back home. How far was that? He had no idea. He just remembered how he'd kept going, day and night, half-asleep sometimes. He might have been a month on the road, or it might have been a year. He couldn't remember and what did it matter anyway? When he got home, his wife had married another man. His elder brother couldn't afford to keep her and thought he was dead. So he sold her, and now Old Man Xinjiang's wife belonged to another man. Old Man Xinjiang hadn't had any money to buy her back again, so that was that. The other man was well off in those days so she went with him, hoping for a better life. That was that. But people kept on asking, on and on…

'That was really hard on you,' said the doctor, 'Just getting one go with her.'

Old Man Xinjiang smiled and thought to himself, I didn't even get that. She had her period.

'Aren't you angry with your brother?'

'What's the point in being angry? You take what life throws at you.'

'Why didn't you marry again?'

'Why bother? You take what life throws at you.'

Old Man Xinjiang squinted at the sky outside the window, at the trees under the sky, and the yellow leaves blowing down in the autumn wind. His face might have been carved out of wood. As if this whole story had nothing to do with him.

The doctor took a look at his arm. 'Undo your trousers,' he said. Old Man Xinjiang pulled his trousers down, revealing a pair of skinny buttocks.

'Give me the jab into the flesh,' he said. 'Last time you hit the bone and I couldn't sit down for a week.'

The doctor laughed. 'You haven't got any flesh,' he said. 'I can only get hold of a few inches of skin, that's all there is. You should feed yourself better, instead of giving every cent you get to her. She's married to someone else. Why are you bothering with her?' Old Man Xinjiang said nothing. 'You take too much on yourself,' the doctor went on. 'It's not doing you any good.'

'There you go again,' Old Man Xinjiang said. 'And you, an educated man...' The doctor pinched the skin and injected him. 'It went into the flesh this time,' said Old Man Xinjiang. 'It only hurt a bit.'

The doctor laughed and slapped his rump as if he were a horse: 'You can get up now, but mind you, don't crack the bed boards with those sharp bones of yours.'

'Ah-ya,' complained Old Man Xinjiang, 'that hurt.'

'Huh,' said the doctor, 'Those old bones of yours ring like a monastery bell.'

Old Man Xinjiang got home and put down his baskets. They were considerably lighter now, and he felt a twinge of annoyance. But he shook it from his head. That's just how it was. You needed to be smart in this life, he thought to himself.

His house was small. There was a *kang* bed and a mud-brick stove, and a tall narrow window. The beams and walls were blackened with smoke, the paper covering the window was yellowed with age and the room was dark. That was the way he liked it. He lived alone. It was cosy and he could shut out the world just by shutting the door. A warm feeling stole over him. This house was good. It kept out the wind and the rain, and there was no one to pester him with such impudent remarks. He was afraid of their remarks. After all these years, he'd put it all behind him. Their remarks brought back the memories and the distress.

Old Man Xinjiang poked the fire, rinsed a yam and cut it into pieces on his chopping board. Yams were good. A few minutes in the pan and they were soft-he could swallow them easily. His teeth had all gone years ago. Chewing other sorts of vegetables was hard work and gave him indigestion. He chopped the yam into largish pieces so they would soften quickly but would be easy to pick up with his chopsticks. His hands did not shake but they were getting clumsy.

The chopping board was a small one, only five inches across. He'd had it for half a lifetime and was used to it. Fruit wood was really good. You could cut anything on it without leaving marks. Chen the carpenter had wanted to make him a new one but he didn't see why he needed another. He was on his own and this one was enough. Over the years, other people changed their chopping boards, but he'd stuck with this one. Yes, fruit wood was really good. After all these years, it had only got a little thinner. That was good too. It made it lighter. Small though it was, it had been heavy. Now he was old, he was glad it was lighter.

When he had finished chopping the yam, he had a look at the stove. This *kang* stove was easy to use, it fired up quickly. He put a small pan on its top and took out the can of oil. He wrapped the chopsticks in a rag, dipped them and oiled the bottom of the pan. It gave off a good smell. This was sesame oil, which he liked better than rapeseed oil. Though when he had no sesame oil, he'd use the rapeseed oil and it smelled just as good. And if that was gone, he did without oil. He always had noodles and yams, so that was all right. Apart from the Three Years of Famine in 1960s, when they hadn't had yams, or anything else, and he'd had to live on sow thistles. Anyway, the good thing was that he hadn't starved to death. So many had. He was lucky. Very lucky. He'd come through without any major illness or other disaster. But then, you take what life throws at you, good or bad...

The house was quite still, the only noise his occasional mumbles. The bits of yam sounded good as they went into the pan. It was a nicer sound than the songs that came over the village loudspeakers. Not that there was anything wrong with those women's voices, but what he really liked was Shaanxi opera, with its high-pitched singing and fiery rhythms. He'd never bought a radio of his own, so he hadn't listened to it for years. But the hissing sound of the hot yam sounded good too. Pity it didn't last long, then you had to add the water. Old Man Xinjiang ladled out a potful of water. That was all he used at each meal. It wasn't a big pot, the size of a bowl, but that amount of water was enough for one meal. It floated in the water-jar all day, bobbing gently from side to side apparently at whim. This was something else he'd had for decades. It had no lip, but that was all right. It had started out with a lip, but one day he'd had it on the stove-top to heat some water, and the cat with the white nose had sent it flying. It was still useful though, as a ladle. His bowl was no good for that because you couldn't get it through the neck of the water jar. But the lip-less pot was fine. It was hard to explain things in this life; a lip-less pot was good for some things and a lipped pot was good for others. And who was to say which use was more important?

The water soon came to the boil. Old Man Xinjiang began to make noodles. He got out a big china bowl. It was thick, heavy and sturdy. You couldn't buy bowls like that in the market any more. Sturdy things had many uses, and he used this bowl both to eat out of and to mix noodle dough in. It saved him buying a special mixing bowl. He put in a scoop of flour and some water and rubbed in the flour. He gave it a quick knead and brought it together in a lump the size of his fist. Then he flattened it onto his chopping board and cut it into long strips with his knife. One by one, he rubbed each strip between his hands to thin it. It was quick work. Simple food never took long to prepare.

He'd eaten like this for several decades.

He was old, really old, and rich food gave him indigestion. He liked plain food with plenty of soupy liquid. You didn't need money for the good things in life. Like a simple meal, like fetching a stool and sitting down to look at the stars and the moon. The sun came up and went down, the leaves of the trees started green and went yellow. They were the good things in life and no one could take them from him.

It was dusk and the darkness crept up on him. Old Man Xinjiang's dinner was cooked and he carried his bowl to the doorway and sat down. He picked out a morsel with his chopsticks and offered it to the guardian spirits. Then he began noisily slurping his noodles. Steam rose from the bowl and up over his head. There was another bowl in front of him on the ground with the same food in it, prepared for a friend the black dog. Just then, the black dog turned up, having made its leisurely way from the woman's house on the east side of the village in the pale moonlight. Noiselessly it lapped its dinner, then raised its head in greeting. This was the time when Old Man Xinjiang felt most contented. He could forget himself, and the dog, and all the villagers.

Beauty

1

Meng Zi and Yue were married. It was a lively occasion, with the menfolk, who'd had plenty to drink, bursting into the couple's room and playing the usual tricks on the bride and groom.

But Meng Zi was in for a shock. On their wedding night, Yue would not let him touch her. Her excuse was that while she was working in Lanzhou, she had used someone else's bowl to wash her private parts and caught beriberi. She didn't want him to get it too. Meng Zi did not believe her. He made her go into town for a check-up when she paid the customary visit back to her parents' home on the third day after the wedding. The doctor had a good look at Yue and told Meng Zi that his wife had syphilis.

Meng Zi was appalled. No wonder she had refused to let him touch her. He thought back to every physical contact he had had with Yue, and he reckoned she must have known all along.

Meng Zi knew quite well what syphilis was. Now he felt a huge sense of injustice and humiliation. He hardly heard what the doctor was telling him. His mind seemed to have gone numb. After a while, he heard the doctor ask: 'Have you had intercourse with your wife?' Meng Zi shook his head. 'Well, that's a good thing,' said the doctor. 'You shouldn't worry too much, in any case. Modern medicine has made great advances, and this disease is treatable.' Meng Zi said nothing. What was going round and round in his head was: How could you do this to me, Yue?

It was all becoming clear…He remembered the times when he had wanted to sleep with her before the wedding, and Yue had said: 'What's the hurry? Wait till we're married, and then I'll be yours.' He had taken that as evidence of Yue's chastity. He had known so many women who were easy. Yue's show of resistance moved him. In his years away from home, he had lived a lot. He knew quite well that love these days was a luxury. He had not remotely guessed that the real reason was that his new bride had syphilis, and knew it. He was in the depths of despair.

The doctor tried to reassure him. 'This disease is extremely infectious. You should be grateful that she held out on you, and you didn't catch it too.'

Meng Zi laughed bitterly. All the same, he realised he'd had had a narrow escape. He no longer blamed Yue so harshly, but his anguish was as acute as ever. He made up his mind: He'd get a divorce. The decision made him feel relieved. At the same time, he could not help asking himself: What would happen to Yue after that?

Yue was sitting on a bench at the far end of the corridor, her head in her hands, looking full of trepidation. Meng Zi went up to her. She did not look up, just shifted along a bit. Meng Zi just said: 'Let's go.' Then he left without waiting to see if she was following.

Outside, it was bright and sunny, in stark contrast to the gloom that filled their hearts. Meng Zi let out a long breath. He thought of his parents and all the money they had paid for his wedding, and was furious with Yue. He halted and turned around. He suddenly noticed how thin she looked. Her clothes hung loose on her. A breeze caught her hair and blew it across her pale, unhappy face. She looked hopelessly frail. Meng Zi softened. He could not leave her to fend for herself. He decided that he would stick around until she was cured of her illness, then get an immediate divorce.

He waited for Yue to catch up and they walked along together. Neither spoke. Around them everything was still, in spite of the usual city noises. They were desolate, each in their own silent, lonely world, and had no desire to talk.

Meng Zi saw how dry Yue's lips were, and bought an ice cream. 'Don't fret about things,' he said, giving it to her. 'We'll get it sorted.' Yue was dumb for a moment, then burst into tears. She began to talk. She had gone to work in Lanzhou when she decided to get out of the village, she told him, but she soon discovered that Lanzhou was not her city. She was a drifter there, with nowhere to go, a bit of pondweed. She had taken a string of jobs but never slept around. Then she was taken up by a businessman from Beijing who promised to marry her. They slept together, and she got syphilis from him. After she got sick, she went through a lot, and it taught her the value of true love as simple country folk experienced it. She went back to the village and threw herself at Meng Zi. She had been treating herself for the syphilis as she made the wedding preparations, confident that she would be cured in time. She would give her all for true love.

Meng Zi listened, feeling a strange sort of calm. He understood exactly what she meant. He had gone looking for labouring jobs in the towns and the mines, and had suffered the pain of being an outsider too. One night, he was wandering the streets, gnawed by feelings of hunger, cold and loneliness. On all sides, the buildings towered above him, their brightly-lit windows looking down like eyes. He could not find any corner to shelter from the cold. He wandered up and down the avenues, under the pale street lighting, counting his footsteps, then counting the time. How could a night drag on for so long? All his time away, he had never stopped feeling like an outsider.

He shook his head, then turned around and saw Yue looking at him. It was exactly the same way his big brother Han Tou had looked at the doctor when he was dying. He suddenly felt a rush of affection, put his arm around her waist and squeezed her tight. She burst into tears.

They were in the town of Liangzhou. In the noise and bustle, no one paid any attention to a woman crying, or a man looking anguished. There were people all around, but Meng Zi felt distanced from them all. His arm still around his wife's waist, he walked on. She was still sobbing. Meng Zi was overwhelmed with pity and tenderness.

He knew now that his fate was forever bound up with this woman.

They strolled along the streets, trying to cheer each other up by putting on a show of enjoying themselves, but it felt phony and they were soon tired of it. Yue stopped smiling and peered into the distance. There was a touch of anxiety in her expression, which accentuated her beauty. If only she wasn't sick, thought Meng Zi, how good things would be. He felt desolate. The most beautiful things in life could be spoiled. He had had high hopes, for a business, for love. And now his wife, the one he had had so many plans for, turned out to have this shameful past. It was not her sickness so much as her affair that he found unbearable. Every time he remembered it, he felt as if he was swallowing foul water. He pushed the thought from his mind, but it kept returning to haunt him. It struck him again that he must get divorced. That would be sweet revenge.

'I'm not a slurry pit for other people's waste,' he thought. People from around here regarded being a 'slurry pit' as the worst thing that could happen to you. It was where the farmers stored their spare sewage when they manured their fields. It was what happened to Jia Baoyu, in the novel *Dream of the Red Chamber*, when Xue Baochai was dashed her hopes of entering the palace, she treated him as her 'slurry pit'.

Yue had only married him because she'd failed to become a proper townswoman. He did not like the thought of being second-best. But no matter how vehemently he told himself he would get a divorce, as soon as he took a look at the woman by his side, he relented. It was that look of helpless despair on her face. Meng Zi thought of his dead brother and how he had looked. Only someone who had really experienced life's hardest knocks looked like that. Meng Zi sighed to himself. Well, they would take it one step at a time.

They did not talk on their way home. Meng Zi tried to think something cheerful to say, but decided silence was best.

Yue gazed out at the scenery flashing by, her face expressionless. Meng Zi thought that life was like the passing scenery. It could change dramatically in a flash. He'd been through a lot in the last few years, life, death, things that had seemed laughing matters that in the end had brought tears…Yue had been so sure she could shake the dust of the village from her feet, but fate had drawn her inexorably back here, to become the wife of a peasant. The word 'wife' gave him a pang. A wife with syphilis-that was not what he had imagined.

Then he thought of his mother, and felt another pang. His mother was proud of her new daughter-in-law. She had been singing her praises all around the village. And now Yue was sick. What a slap in the face for their ancestors. What a come-down for his mother. Meng Zi felt that Yue's family must have known all along they were giving him a maggot. What an underhand thing for them to do. He was livid.

2

They got to Yue's home. The anxious look her mother gave

Meng Zi convinced him that she knew exactly what was wrong with her daughter. They had all been in cahoots. It was obvious. Somehow, the illness now took second place to the deception. That was what was making him so angry. How could they have married her off, knowing that she was ill, he asked himself? He could not bring himself to greet his in-laws.

Yue's mother looked at her daughter, then at her son-in-law. She opened her mouth to speak, but no words came out. Meng Zi got in first. 'You carry on, I'm off home,' he said. The custom was for bride and groom to return to the bride's home on the third day and stay there for three days. Meng Zi would be expected to stay with her, but he could not bear to. They had made a complete fool of him. He decided to go back home.

As he went out, he turned, to see Yue leaning against the white poplar, gazing after him. He softened again, and felt the tears come. He would have liked to go back and stay with Yue, but he couldn't stand her mother's attitude. Eventually he turned the corner and walked away.

His mother was at their gate, busy with her chores. 'Have you eaten?' she greeted Meng Zi. He did not want to tell her that they had been to town, so he just said: 'The food was too greasy. It didn't agree with me. I'll just have some noodles and greens.' His mother threw down her tools and went into the kitchen to cook him some noodles.

He watched his mother as he ate them. She was thinner, but she looked tougher than ever. She washed her sweaty face and it shone apple-red. Meng Zi thought of Yue's illness and felt a pang.

After dinner, he went for a lie-down, feeling depressed. Everything in their new room mocked him. His pity for Yue evaporated, and he was angry again. It was unforgiveable, he thought. Anything else he could have forgiven, but not this. What a vile thing to do to him. The thought of divorce floated to the top of his mind again.

He could not rest. After a while, he thought he might as well get up. He left the house and went to the fields.

The fields were full of people working. There were a few jokey comments as he passed, but his responses were absent-minded. He walked up to the ridge. From here he could see White Tiger Pass. In the few days he had been away, it had sprouted yet more new buildings and red flags. He had heard that a businessman wanted to buy up some land and build a resort in the desert, with a camel-racing arena and stuff. A place like this was a new fad for city folk, apparently, now they had had their fill of eating, drinking and the bright lights of the city. That was all very well, but what difference would a glitzy new town actually make? He could not be bothered to walk further. He found a place to hunker down and let his thoughts wander.

Suddenly, Yue appeared in the fields. She had been home to find him, and followed him out here. Some of the farmers greeted her, and she greeted them back, as cheerfully as she always did. Meng Zi frowned at the sound of her voice. Heartless bitch! he thought. Then it occurred to him that she did not want anyone knowing there was anything wrong.

Feng Xiang exchanged a few words with her and pointed in Meng Zi's direction. As she ran towards him, her face lit up with joy. No doubt she was putting that on too. But it was real, he realised. She was like a lost child who had finally found its mother. A wave of emotion flooded over Meng Zi.

'Without you, I didn't want to stay there any longer,' she explained to him when she'd caught her breath. 'Don't make fun of me!' Meng Zi, suddenly tender, seized her hands. She held them tight, as if afraid she might fly away.

'What a scene!' Feng Xiang shouted from a distance. 'Aren't you afraid people will tease you?'

Yue stuck out her tongue in embarrassment and, dropping his hands, moved away a little. The sun was going down in the west, and big clouds gusted across the sky. There was a pungent smell in the air, perhaps slurry from the pits on White Tiger Pass. Meng Zi looked at Yue and tenderness welled in his heart. It was always like that when he looked at her.

They found a clean bit of ground and sat down. 'You've got to get treatment straightaway,' said Meng Zi. 'You've got to pull this disease out by its roots. That means a stay in hospital. If we don't have enough money, I'll borrow some.' 'I have a bit put by,' said Yue. 'And I'll get a bit more from my dad. I'll say we've got relatives to visit in town. Then I'll check into hospital. So far, I've only been to private clinics, and they told me it wasn't serious. A few pills would sort it. They took my money off me, but the pills didn't cure me.'

'We won't tell my mum and dad,' said Meng Zi. This was something he had to deal with on his own.

'Once I'm better,' said Yue, 'I really will be yours.' And she went scarlet. Meng Zi looked at her beautiful face, and his heart skipped a beat. He took her in his arms and kissed her hard.

When the post-wedding visit to her parents was over, Yue and Meng Zi returned to his parents' home. The wedding decorations were still up, giving it a festive atmosphere, but Meng Zi was heavy-hearted. Although syphilis was not supposed to be fatal, still, it had killed off some feeling he nurtured deep inside him. He was torn between trepidation and anger; annoyance with Yue and love for her. He tried to keep smiling, but his mother saw through him. 'What's up?' she asked. 'If you've got a problem, spit it out.' Meng

Zi had just been thinking of an excuse to get Yue into hospital for treatment. Now he said: 'It's like this. Yue wants to go to town to see an uncle and aunt and she wants me with her.' 'Well, go if you want to,' said his mother. 'Don't make yourself ill fretting about it.'

The next day, Meng Zi went to White Tiger Pass, to the pit he was working in, and said he'd be off for three weeks at least. Then, relieved, he set off with Yue and she checked into Liangzhou Hospital.

3

A couple of weeks later, Yue was still not responding to treatment. She was allergic to penicillin and cephalosporin antibiotics. The drugs she could tolerate produced no result. The doctor said she should have come earlier. The syphilis was at advanced stage. They had better try the big hospital in Lanzhou City, and see if they could do anything for her. Yue protested that she had been getting treatment. It was just that the alternatives to antibiotics had made little difference. Meng Zi was distraught. The doctor tried to reassure him: 'Don't worry. At least it's not AIDS. Syphilis is not such a big deal nowadays.' 'Right,' said Yue. 'Some people get it much worse than me and get cured. Dad consulted an old Chinese herbalist who specializes in syphilis. They say he works miracles.'

They checked out and Meng Zi took Yue to see the old herbalist. According to Yue, he was a master of Taoist *fengshui*. There were stories that, in the old days before 1949, a rain-maker in Liangzhou Town (a Taoist priest himself) used to consult him before signing a contract to make rain in drought years. The county government drove a hard bargain: He got 500 *dan*(50kg) of grain if he succeeded. If he failed, they could burn him to death. So, first, the rain-maker consulted Old Man Liang, the herbalist. Liang made a few calculations on his fingers, then predicted exactly which day that rain would next fall. And the rain-maker signed the contract for that day. If Liang told the rain-maker that there would be no rain in the near future, then the rain-maker would not do the deal, no matter how much grain the county government offered him. Nowadays, Old Man Liang was consulted by roast-chicken sellers, when they had surplus to get rid of and wanted to know a good place. Whichever direction he pointed them to, they went, and always sold out. Liang still worked as a doctor too, specializing in alchemy. He could cure all sorts of diseases, much worse ones than syphilis.

Yue seemed very confident.

But Meng Zi was still heavy-hearted. She was just trying to comfort him. He noticed she often cried, though she hid it from him. So, he too put a brave face on it.

Liang was a sallow-faced old man, with a perfectly smooth, whiskerless chin. The only thing that marked him as out of the ordinary were his enormous fleshy ears, almost elephant-shaped. Meng Zi was sceptical that he was as effective as he was made out to be. Yue however was enthusiastic.

The old man showed no emotion. He did not ask about Yue's symptoms. He just told her to take off her jacket and top and fetched out a small ball, stuck around with needles like a pincushion. He selected some and inserted them into Yue's back, which was soon covered in drops of blood. 'Does it hurt?' asked Meng Zi. Yue said no. Liang went on inserting needles until he had used forty or fifty. Then he got a bottle and sprinkled a yellow powder over the blood drops.

By the time the session was over, Yue was covered in sweat, but looked brighter than before. She gave the old doctor some money, which he left lying on the table. 'You've got to keep up the treatment if you want a cure,' he said. Yue smiled apologetically. 'I was afraid it would hurt. But from now on, I'll keep coming.'

They took the packets of herbs the old man gave them, thanked him and left. Yue was excited. 'I've been to him before, and I did get better. I only stopped coming because the treatment was so painful. If I'd kept it up, I'd have been better ages ago.' She sounded regretful. 'Better a short pain than a long one,' said Meng

Zi. 'Keep up the treatment this time. I'll get hold of a scooter and bring you every day.' 'You don't need to do that,' said Yue. 'I only have to come once a week. The other days, I can wash myself with the herbal infusion.'

They got on the bus for home, dropping in at the karaoke bar in White Tiger Pass to pick up the shopping they had left there. That was so that they could keep it from Meng Zi's mother that Yue had been in the hospital. Her father was in the bar, chatting to a friend, and greeted his daughter affectionately. Meng Zi was cool towards his father-in-law. He was still furious that Yue's family had collectively deceived him. Yue's dad seemed unconcerned, and got him a drink.

'How's business?' Yue asked. 'Not as good as before. There's competition, with the new bars, and if you don't have decent girls, you don't get the customers.' Meng Zi was infuriated by this comment. 'I'm off,' he said, banging down his drink. What he wanted to say was, You beast! Your daughter's ruined and you're still trying to ruin other girls.

Yue came running after him. 'Did you hear him?' he demanded. 'He's still looking for girls!' Yue was silent. Then she said: 'Don't blame Dad for what happened to me. I did that myself.' 'But he made you go and work in a bar, didn't he?' Yue gave a long sigh. 'Well, all I can say is, the city's full of girls who've picked up venereal diseases or do drugs, and Dad didn't have anything to do with it. It was always going to happen to me. The temptations were always there. The world is full of temptations. It's easy to make a mistake.' Meng Zi could not argue with that, and fell silent.

Meng Zi's mother was at home when they arrived. She was alarmed to see that Yue was thinner than ever. 'Is she pregnant?' she asked Meng Zi quietly. He felt a pang, but forced a smile: 'Don't be in such a hurry!'

Meng Zi's mother soon discovered what was wrong with her daughter-in-law.

The next morning, before she went off to the fields, she pushed open their bedroom door to have a word with Meng Zi—to find Yue squatting over a bowl and washing herself by the light of a torch. Meng Zi had deliberately left their bedroom door unlocked. It was his way of ensuring that he did not get carried away and go too far with Yue. Horrified, Yue grabbed some toilet paper to cover herself.

The old woman called Meng Zi out of the room. She looked as if she had seen a ghost. 'Tell me the truth!' she demanded. 'Is it the pox?' Meng Zi just smiled. 'Don't talk nonsense!' 'Oh god, what have I done to deserve this?' His mother groaned. The tears began to roll down her cheeks. She struggled to control them, but the more she wiped them away, the more the tears flowed.

'Mum, you were imagining things,' Meng Zi tried again.

'I haven't lived all these years without knowing what's what. One of Yue's aunts got sick that way. It's just the same, I saw it. And now she's made you sick too.' She burst into a storm of tears.

Meng Zi had to come clean. 'There's nothing wrong with me. I haven't touched her,' he reassured her. His mother stopped crying. 'Really?' Meng Zi nodded. His mother embraced him and cried even harder.

Meng Zi felt terribly sad, but at the same time, relieved. It was better for his parents to know. They would have found out sooner or later anyway.

His mother wiped her tears. 'I'm not interfering, son,' she said. 'I just want to say that if you ever touch that pus, that's the end of you.' Then she burst out furiously: 'Yue's father! That beast! He knew his daughter was sick and he thought he'd make my son sick too!'

Meng Zi, worried that Yue would be upset, tried to hush her: 'No one's trying to make anyone sick. It wasn't intentional.' He felt far from forgiving towards Yue's parents however.

At that point, old Shun came in. 'What on earth's up now, you old nag?' he reproved his wife. 'You're always making such a song and dance about things.' The old woman blew her nose. 'You've got yourself a fine daughter-in-law,' she said. 'she's brought the pox with her.' Old Shun looked at his son, startled. Meng Zi explained what had happened. He was afraid that his father would be furious, because he had always been against his marriage to Yue but, to his surprise, he just gave a dark look at the bedroom door, then at his son, and said nothing. He sat down on the steps, and mechanically lit his pipe.

It was very quiet. The sun was half-way above the horizon and just taking a peek into the courtyard. Meng Zi's mother wiped her nose a few times.

Meng Zi went back to the bedroom, where Yue was sitting numbly on the edge of the *kang* bed. Meng Zi wished she would have a good cry too, like his mother. She might have felt a little better. But she just sat there blankly. The stillness in the room felt unbearably oppressive. On the floor, sat the bowl full of yellowish water, some squares of toilet paper, and the medicine bottle, with flecks of yellow powder in it.

Yue sat like a statue. Meng Zi could not think what to say to her. He gave a long sigh. His parents' anguish…Yue's despair…He understood both only too well. They were all hurting. But who was to blame?

He touched her shoulder gently. 'They were going to find out sooner or later.'

At this, Yue burst into floods of tears. As she struggled to get herself under control, her whimpers made Meng Zi's heart ache. He screwed the cap on the bottle, picked up the paper and pushed the bowl under a chair. He could not go and empty it. He was too afraid of upsetting his mother again. She had not laboured to bring him into the world, just to see their piss-pot full of 'poxy' water.

Yue wiped her eyes: 'Don't blame Mum and Dad. They didn't want me to marry you, but I insisted. I never thought the disease would be so hard to get rid of.'

'No more talking. I'm not blaming you.' Meng Zi put his arm around her, then went outside. The courtyard was filled with sunlight. Chickens were busy pecking for grain. His father sat motionless, holding his pipe.

His mother was nowhere to be seen. Meng Zi, suddenly afraid she had gone to see Yue's parents, hurried after her.

5

On her way, the old woman cursed and swore. She was seething with rage. 'What a disaster! What monsters!' The village had emptied as business picked up at White Tiger Pass. It was so quiet that the few kids playing in the street overheard. They knew that her thunderous expression meant trouble and tagged along behind her, aping her expression and repeating her curses.

'You monster!' She meant Yue's mother. Passing off a

syphilitic slut as a marriageable girl was worse than peddling fake medicine. Never mind the wedding gifts, if her boy really had caught syphilis then Yue's mother had as good as killed him. You monster! You beast! You cow! You bitch! She called the woman all the vituperative names she could think of, but she was still seething with hatred.

She kicked up eddies of dust until her trouser legs were white with it, as she hurried along the road, ignoring the villagers' greetings. They exchanged glances, then turned and followed her. If there was a big drama in the offing, no one wanted to miss it.

The gate to Yue's family's smallholding hung ajar. Meng Zi's mother gave it a fierce kick and stormed in. Yue's mother heard the crash, and knew it was not good news. But she put on a smile anyway and greeted her fellow mother-in-law politely.

'You monster! What a terrible thing to do!' Shun's missus yelled at her. She pulled off her shoe, and before Yue's mother had time to react, whacked her hard across the face with it. The other woman did her best to dodge out of the way, until she heard the words: 'You wretch! Giving us the pox!' Then she curled up on the ground, unresisting, and let the other woman beat her across the face. The blows covered her face with dust, then drew blood which trickled from her mouth.

If Yue's mother had fought back, Meng Zi's mother would

probably have beaten her all the harder. But she did not. Instead, she almost seemed to offer her face up to the blows raining down on her. Meng Zi's mother began to feel ridiculous. She put her shoe back on, picked up a stone and went into the house: 'I'm going to smash up this pox-ridden house!' There were sounds of breaking glass, shattering wood, and a prolonged wail.

'You monster! You monster! What did you think you were doing, giving your poxy daughter to us?' Meng Zi's mother was cursing and keening as if she was a funeral-wailer.

Yue's mother sat blankly on the doorstep, her face and clothes covered in dirt. Her eyes were sunken, like two dried-up wells. She had always been a formidable character. The villagers had never seen her looking so wretched. Once upon a time, she would have given as good as she got in a fight. That would have made a fine drama. But the disappointed villagers had at least learnt something new: Yue had the pox.

Meng Zi did not expect his mother to have a go at Yue's mother in public, until he heard the commotion. He arrived at Yue's home to find the entrance packed with people. Furious, he realised that the fuss his mother had made had left his wife's reputation in tatters. He pushed the onlookers aside and saw his mother-in-law sitting wretchedly in the courtyard. He rushed to pull her to her feet. He had to get her into the house. They could talk there. But the old woman just slumped on the ground. Every tug he gave only made her wail louder. She banged her head on the ground so hard that her forehead came up black and blue.

'What are you laughing at?' demanded Meng Zi, rounded on the curious villagers clustered round the courtyard entrance. At that, two of them came in to help him pull her to her feet.

Meng Zi went inside, and saw the shattered mirror glass on the floor. The tabletop had several more holes in it and the chipboard showed through. He sighed with frustration. He knew this was his mother's handiwork.

She sat on the *kang* bed, keening and wailing at the top of her voice, stopping only to curse 'the pox!' She was sitting on a red satin quilt she had found. It was covered in dirt-she had made it filthy. Meng Zi suddenly felt as if his head was exploding. How could she have done this? The village women often made a big drama about things, but not his mother. He had only once seen her lose control like this: when he was a small boy, he had been given a bloody nose by a much bigger boy. She had dragged him off to see the parents and given them a right telling-off. Right now, her rage seemed to have sent her round the bend.

'What have you done, mother?' Meng Zi said, tears of rage in his own eyes.

'What have I done? I didn't pass off a pox-ridden girl as a

bride!' she shrieked.

'Please, mum, stop making such a fuss!' Meng Zi beseeched her. 'The way you're going on, this will be the end of her!'

'What she did was nearly the end of you! We spent all that money on the wedding and all you bought was the pox!'

Meng Zi sighed. Then he felt a spurt of anger. Couldn't she have been a bit more considerate to him? This girl she was bad-mouthing was her daughter-in-law, his wife. But his mother was oblivious to his feelings, and he was powerless to do anything about that. He was also worried about the damage to Yue. Now that his mother had told the whole village, if Yue appeared here again, they would shower her with spit.

At that moment, Yue's brother, White Dog turned up, looking belligerent. He was spoiling for a fight and glared at Meng Zi. In a few words, Meng Zi explained what had happened, and White Dog turned his rage on his mother instead. 'Damn and blast you, mother!' he yelled.

Then he turned to the curious onlookers: 'And what do you think you're looking at?' he demanded. They slunk away.

White Dog rounded on his mother again. 'I thought you were up to no good. I heard all that whispering. So this is what it was all about! You've brought shame on the ancestors! You've got to back out. Back out of the marriage. Get the girl back. Feed her to the dogs!'

The two women set up another chorus of wails. There was still whispering coming from outside. This should have been a private family affair. Instead, the whole village knew about it. Meng Zi felt strangely calm. 'Why hide it away?' he thought. It wasn't such a big deal, after all.

The trouble was that Yue would be overwhelmed by all the fuss. How could she show her face after this?

6

The villagers were on Meng Zi's side. His mother went along with them for starters, until she gradually began to feel she'd been in the wrong, although she didn't want to admit it out loud. In the end, Yue's family paid back the 10,000 yuan they'd received as a wedding gift. Meng Zi's parents didn't mention their wedding gifts. They just said that the girl should get medical treatment.

Meng Zi's mother knew that they'd got the money back because she'd made a fuss, but she also knew it was at Yue's expense. Everyone was gossiping about it. It was all over the village. And every time it was mentioned, someone would spit in the direction of Yue's home. Someone even suggested dragging the girl off to the clan temple to suffer public criticism for having made their ancestors lose face. What held them back in the end, however, was White Dog's unpredictable temper.

The villagers reckoned that the syphilis was all down to a girl leaving home. Yue's father's sister had caught it too, when she worked as a hooker in a big hotel out west before Liberation. Syphilis was her punishment and she had died wretchedly. They didn't know of anyone else who worked in this line of business. In recent years, so many girls had gone off as migrant workers, but no one knew where the money they sent home came from, because most of them changed their names and worked far from home. There was no proof one way or the other that they were no longer quite as clean-living as they had been. With Yue, there was cast-iron proof: She'd caught the pox. And that shamed her forever. The villagers even muttered that Meng Zi had caught it too. If you got too close to the flame, you'd get burned. They didn't believe that Meng Zi could hold that gorgeous girl in his arms and still stay chaste. The village women kept out of Meng Zi's way as if afraid he might give them the pox just by looking at them. And that went for the ugliest old hags too.

It finally dawned on Meng Zi's mother what damage she had done to her son's reputation by making such a public scene. Even if he got a divorce, no girl would dare marry him after this. So she dropped the idea of a divorce, and concentrated on getting Yue better. They would use the money Yue's family had sent back and throw a bit of science at that damned pox.

Without admitting she had been in the wrong, she made her peace with her son and daughter-in-law. She convinced her husband old Shun to spend 800 yuan on an old motorbike so that Meng Zi could ride Yue to Liangzhou City, for treatment at old man Liang's clinic.

Old Shun decided not to send Meng Zi back to White Tiger Pass. Unluckily, a bunch of gold-panners turned up claiming that Meng Zi owed them more than 3,000 yuan. Old Shun was mortified, but Meng Zi drew himself up to his full height and swore he'd pay them back himself. He was grown-up now and his father could say nothing, although he was secretly very sore about it for a long time afterwards.

When Meng Zi brought his bedding back from his shack up at the mine workings, his mum and dad were frantic. It was different when he was keeping his shop and living separately from Yue. Now they were living and sleeping together, and the syphilis hung like a sword of Damocles over everyone's head. It was true he said that he had never touched Yue, but that was different from saying he never would touch her in the future. He was a red-blooded young man, after all. They were in dread that he might get carried away one day and get off with his wife. …and come into contact with the pox.

The old couple were constantly on edge. They kept on at their son to be on his guard. And they imposed a rule: He and Yue were not allowed to lock their bedroom door when they went to bed at night. Meng Zi's mother and father agreed that they would take it in turn to stay up at night and tiptoe across barefoot and eavesdrop, when the young couple's light went out. If they heard anything going on, they would sound the alarm. At first, old Shun reckoned that was not just mean, it was very unjust. But he gave in when he saw his wife staying up on her own, and they split the hours between them.

Meng Zi had no idea that he and Yue were under surveillance.

The first night, Yue washed herself, dabbed on the medicinal powder, pulled on clean trousers and got onto the *kang* bed. The syphilis had not got any worse, but neither was there any marked improvement. They talked about it, and wondered if Yue should go to Lanzhou City Hospital for treatment. Yue was hesitant because she had heard that they used the same medicines as in Liangzhou Town. They talked about other things, remembering the good times when they had been at school. Yue seemed cheerful. She was as pretty as ever, in spite of having grown thinner. In fact she was even more beautiful in Meng Zi's eyes, because his love was mixed with pity. Under the covers, he reached and gripped her hand. Suddenly he was overcome by sadness. His beautiful wife was as unattainable to him as if she was a million miles away.

'Don't sigh like that,' said Yue. 'You can do what you want with me when I'm cured. I'm only afraid you'll have lost interest when the time comes.'

'I'll be happy just so long as you don't beg for mercy!' said Meng Zi. And Yue giggled.

As they chatted on, Meng Zi felt Yue's palm grow sweaty. He tightened, then loosened, his grip. The slippery sensation was tantalizing and he leaned over to kiss Yue. Their lips met...and stayed together. Lips nibbled lips, and tongues entwined. It so happened it was old Shun on 'night duty'. The noises he heard worried him and he crept back to the bedroom. Waking his wife, he said: 'There's something going on.' Throwing a jacket over her shoulders, she rushed to the other bedroom door. 'Meng Zi!' she cried. 'What?' 'Come and find some pain-killers for your father. He's got a headache.' Meng Zi hastily got out of bed, switched on the torch, and did as he was told. He put the medicine in a glass of water and gave it to his father. It gave his mother a chance to exhort him again to 'stay away from her! The pus is so infectious!' 'I know, I know,' said Meng Zi. His father was reassured by his tone of voice, but his mother was still in a state of anxiety. She put on more clothes and took over 'night duty'.

The kiss they had exchanged aroused both of them. Just a

kiss, but so pleasurable. Apart, they were separate, embraced, they became part of each other. It was blissful, but also frustrating. They began to caress each other, making sure to keep their trousers on, to avoid getting carried away and going too far. Then they stripped off and lay naked to the waist, in each other's arms.

It felt wonderful, but Meng Zi felt he was on a slippery slope. They had started holding hands, then progressed to kissing, then embracing, skin-to-skin. He was becoming more and more aroused.

The noises she was hearing had his mother in a high state of anxiety. Meanwhile, Meng Zi and Yue had no idea they were being spied on, or that their pleasures were putting his parents into such a panic.

Meng Zi was finding his arousal acutely painful. Yue's body was forbidden fruit, but his own body was not going to listen to reason forever. He felt like he was going to explode. Yue was by nature soft and yielding, and began to moan with every caress. She did not know if she was doing this to please Meng Zi or whether she simply could not help it, but the effect on Meng Zi was as much painful as pleasurable. Old Shun, on guard outside the door, was appalled. 'You slut!' he kept muttering. He listened to the noises with a sort of fearful fascination, sweat beading on his forehead.

Yue and Meng Zi had hardly been apart for a moment during the weeks of her treatment, but his kisses were her first chance to enjoy feeling like a woman. The fact that consummating that passion was an unattainable prospect only intensified their feelings.

The moonlight coming in through the curtains filled the small room with a mysterious pale light which rippled gently over Yue's body. Meng Zi found her indescribably beautiful. Yue gazed at him with quietly sorrowful eyes, trying to control the heaving of her bosom as her fingers traced Meng Zi's body. He sucked her small breasts, inflamed by their soft roundness. In a frenzy of excitement, he threw himself on top of Yue, kissing her passionately. If he could only be one with her, he would be happy to die. Yue resisted only briefly. Meng Zi got out a condom. 'Just once,' he panted. 'I'll wear this.' Yue shook her head frantically and tried to protest: 'No, no!' But then she acquiesced.

His blood pounding in his ears, his mouth parched, Meng Zi tore open the plastic wrapper and something soft dropped into his hand. Yue was about to make him very happy.

Suddenly, there was a cry from his mother: 'Meng Zi! Someone's breaking into the yard!'

Yue realised that her mother-in-law had been keeping watch. She burst into tears like an accidentally scalded child. Meng Zi wept too. They lay sobbing in each other's arms till daybreak.

7

While Yue continued her treatment with old man Liang, her mother-in-law went in search of country remedies. She found it hard to broach the subject with the villagers, who knew almost nothing about it though they all agreed it was filthy. So Meng Zi's mother just asked her close friends. They passed the news on to other people, and Yue quickly became known as a 'slut', but at least their enquiries had the hoped-for result. A herbalist called Acne Wang came up with a remedy: You smoked the infected area with burning ox dung. 'The smoke cures some sufferers if they've just caught the pox,' he said. 'It contains the essence of all kinds of healing grass and flowers that the oxen eat.'

Meng Zi's mother had no idea what essences ox dung contained, but at least the remedy didn't cost anything. There were plenty of families with oxen in the village, and every ox dropped dung. If you smeared the sloppy turds on a wall, in a few days, they dried into pancakes which could be burned. The old woman made a pile of these pancakes and stacked them in a wash bowl. Yue did not think much of the idea. She could not see how smoke was more healing than medical remedies. But eventually her mother-in-law's enthusiasm wore her down. She made Meng Zi leave the house- there was no way she would allow him to see the suppurating sores.

Once Meng Zi had left, Yue dropped her trousers and showed the older woman. Her genitals were covered in deep ulcers which exuded yellow pus. Meng Zi's mother was appalled. She had hated Yue, at the start, for not having done the decent thing. Now, a wave of pity swept over her. She lit the dried dung and gently fanned the sparks until flames took hold and produced eddies of dense pale smoke. That smoke gave her hope. She watched as Yue squatted over the bowl, and the pus formed droplets which dripped, hissing, into the fire.

'Does it hurt?' she asked.

'It's fine.'

Yue, squatting over the flames, felt satisfied as the loathsome pus was consumed by the fire. She seemed to hear a gnashing of teeth and cries of pain from the pus demons. Besides, at the start, the warmth was comforting. Then it began to hurt, although even then, the scorching feeling was almost pleasant. It made her feel slightly dizzy, as if the fire was drawing her down into it, and she would turn into a blue flame herself. 'Go! Get lost!' She told the pus demons, 'Otherwise, I'll be consumed along with you.'

She squatted lower over the flames, and the pus burned more fiercely. A stench filled the room. Yue felt the flames burning her skin. She was not just being smoked, she was being roasted. Now she was impatient to burn up this disease and give her beloved what he wanted. The look of longing in Meng Zi's eyes had made her heart ache.

Her mother-in-law covered the tops of her thighs with a towel to protect them, and told her to raise herself higher. 'It's the smoke that does you good,' she said. 'If you burn your skin, you'll make things worse.' She added more dung pats to the bowl. She had somehow completely forgotten how she had once disapproved of this girl. Now she felt as anguished as if it was her own daughter who was ill.

After a while, she carried the bowl outside and quenched the fire. Yue dabbed herself with toilet paper and pulled her trousers up. She lay down on the bed, feeling exhausted. Her skin hurt a little from the heat, but she was happy. Finally she had a cure, and it cost nothing. She had felt for so long that there was no hope for her, no way forward. At the beginning it was different: She had been optimistic, science was so advanced that there was no disease it couldn't cure. She had been confident enough to marry Meng Zi, continuing the treatment as she made preparations for the wedding. She would be better before then, she was sure. But the ulcers had spread inexorably outwards. If she had known that before, she might have done things differently.

She lay in bed, looking lazily up at the ceiling, where the plastic weddings garlands hung. She remembered Meng Zi's kisses and caresses. Their feelings for each other made just ordinary kisses something extraordinary, she thought. She found it impossible to imagine the happiness they would enjoy when she was cured. She envisaged them being sucked into and swallowed up by a whirlpool of bliss. She smiled.

Meng Zi came in. 'Any better?' he asked. Yue said nothing, just looked at him. He had got thinner. 'Don't be in such a hurry,' she complained. Then she put her arms around him and pressed him to her breasts. She felt a surge of almost motherly love for him. She stroked his face, smoothing his skin gently over and over.

The experience of being pushed down the mineshaft as a punishment for stealing ore-rock had changed Meng Zi. He remembered the helpless, lonely chill, the sense of spiritual desolation, and could not help wondering about the meaning of life. Why was he alive at all, he puzzled? The more he thought, the more life seemed to lose its meaning. Every living thing and creature ended up as a great nothingness in the end, he felt. It was a depressing thought. Still, it was comforting to feel that, on the way to nothingness, he had a woman at his side who would go through life with him, sharing his happiness and his sorrow, dispelling his loneliness.

All this thinking was so pointless. He envied his parents' generation. They had few wants and were satisfied with little. Nowadays people called them ignorant, but weren't they really the wise ones?

The trouble was, he could not turn into his parents, just like he could not go back inside the womb again. He knew there was no cure for the pain his soul felt. If only there was some wise hand who could come and massage his soul, the way Yue stroked his body.

8

Meng Zi's mother decided to send Yue back home to her parents.

The old couple were exhausted. They had sent several letters to Lan Lan at the saltpans, asking her to come home and help them out. But there was no answer. They could not take any more. They worked in the fields by day, and kept watch over their son and daughter-in-law by night. And the night shift was hard work: The slightest stirring made them feel as if they were in a standoff with the enemy. They were living on their nerves. But that was secondary to their fear that, one way or another, whether in a burst of passion, or befuddled by sleep, the deed would be done and that would be that. Yue had to go home. The marriage could be consummated once she was well again.

Old Shun was also thinking about finding his son a job to do so that he did not have too much time on his hands. It so happened

that the city Forestry Department was in the process of setting up a
Fauna and Flora Preservation Centre in Pig's Belly Well. They had
heard that Meng Zi knew the area well and asked if he would agree
to spend a few days there helping out. It was the perfect solution.
Meng Zi was still hesitant but his father immediately agreed. The
old couple breathed a sigh of relief.

Yue burst into floods of tears at the news. Her mother-in-law
assured her that it was only a temporary separation, just to make
sure that there would be no mishaps. It was not like she was being
sent home in disgrace, as village girls sometimes were. They were
not angry with her. They just begged her not to infect their son.
They would still do their bit to make sure that Yue got her treatment,
and would still treat her as their daughter-in-law. But no matter how
much they tried to comfort Yue, she was inconsolable.

They got Feng Xiang over to try and make Yue see sense, but
all she did was cry just as hard. In any case, whatever she said,
Yue did not want to hear it. Good advice just made her feel worse.
Previously, when life had been hard, Feng Xiang had always
secretly envied Yue her carefree life out in the big wide world. Now
that carefree life had trapped Yue. She did not envy her at all.

The girls sat together, silently weeping. It seemed ironic that
Yue's new home was so nice. Its festive colours were in stark
contrast to their gloom. Eventually Feng Xiang wiped her tears and

said: 'Try not to think too much about it. Concentrate on getting better.' 'I've got a bad feeling about this,' said Yue tearfully. 'If I go now, I'm afraid I'll never come back.' 'Rubbish,' said her friend. Yue just shook her head and cried some more.

Meng Zi's mother couldn't bear Yue's crying. It wasn't that she didn't cry herself, but she didn't bother other people with it. Too much weeping and wailing brought bad luck, in the shape of the weeping demon. She knew there was a weeping demon around right now. It always appeared when it heard tears, and it was evil. It could send the family mad. But every time she wanted to try and persuade Yue to stop, Meng Zi said: 'Let her cry. She'll feel better after.'

Tears or no tears, Yue was packed off home by her mother-in-law.

Meng Zi took her after their midday meal. He knew that his parents only wanted what was right for them. Also, he felt he was slipping into something he had never experienced before. He was afraid that when it came to it, he would not be able to keep himself under control. If his mother had not cried out that night, who knows what trouble there would have been. It made him afraid just thinking back on it. He knew the most important thing now was to get Yue better. He was secretly getting together as much money as he could, so that he could take her to Lanzhou City Hospital. He would do everything in his power. And then it would be up to fate.

They walked along the track to Yue's village. People chatting by the roadside gave them a wide berth when they saw it was Yue. Meng Zi was worried, and tried to distract her by changing the subject, but Yue still looked pained. But she had stopped crying. Putting a brave face on it, she marched determinedly forward. Meng Zi understood and did not mention it. Instead, he just chatted about anything that came into his head.

The mask fell as soon as they got to Yue's home and she threw herself into her mother's arms. They both wept. Meng Zi explained his parents' thinking. He tried to put it as positively as he could, but Yue's mother still looked enraged, although she said nothing. She knew her family hadn't a leg to stand on. If Meng Zi brought up divorce again, she wouldn't have dared protest.

When it was time for Meng Zi to leave, Yue got upset again. She clung to his hand as tightly as if he were a lifeline. Meng Zi found her insistence very distressing. He was quite well aware that he was her only mainstay. She was too frail to face the terrors of her illness alone. He heaved a sigh. He felt he had been cruel when he agreed to take her back home.

The house was quiet. Yue's elder brother, White Dog, had gone off to White Tiger Pass. He had paid off the money he owed and had to go back to work as a 'pit-rat' again. Their father was still running the karaoke bar. The whole village was emptied of all but the elderly and children. The family courtyard looked lonely and bare, bleached white by the sun which hung overhead in solitary splendour.

Yue was thinner than ever, her face pale and bloodless. With no one to see her, she stopped putting on a show of bravery and looked frail and wan. Her grip on Meng Zi's arm, however, was surprisingly strong, as if all her remaining strength was concentrated in her hand. She did not want Meng Zi to leave. Her eyes were pitiful, filled with longing.

Impulsively, Meng Zi wished he could rip the disease from Yue's body and take it into himself.

9

Yue left the house and walked to Sandy River. There were plenty of pit-rats in White Tiger Pass who knew there was a girl with syphilis in the village, but she didn't care about pointing fingers. She was going to wait for Meng Zi. He was due back today. He came back every couple of days, each time bringing medicine with him, as well as news from the city. And he brought happiness to Yue.

Yue missed Meng Zi more and more. Truth be told, at the start, what she liked about him was his dependability, so unlike devious city folk. She'd have been hard put to say that she loved him. That crept up on her, quite suddenly, after they got married. Perhaps her guilty conscience was the catalyst or, more likely, they had come to depend on each other. After she fell ill, she had realised that so many things she used to be concerned about were irrelevant. All she wanted now was to seek consolation, alone, with Meng Zi. She saw his face twitch every time she gasped with pain, and saw the sweat break out. That she found truly moving.

Although of course she wanted to get better, most of all, she wanted to see Meng Zi. The minutes and hours crept by, so slowly they seemed like years. The villagers hardly ever dropped by, probably afraid they might catch the pox off her. The house felt oppressive. There was a heavy smell of cinders from the *kang* bed, because the fire-place underneath had not been cleaned out for many years. She spent her time burning ox dung and squatting over the smoke. It was effective. Some of the ulcers were already dry and scabbing over. She went into town once a week, so that Old Man Liang could stick his needles in and raise blood drops all over her back. And apart from swallowing handfuls of big pills, that was all she did. But at least the infection no longer seemed so virulent. Her hopes revived.

When she stepped out of doors, the hostility, especially of the women, was palpable. They were afraid that this 'slut' would seduce their own menfolk, and give them the pox. Yue felt like laughing.

Sometimes she met men too, on her walk. If they were from her clan, they avoided her because she had brought shame on the family. Men with different surnames did not avoid her. They came close and scrutinized her face, as if they were looking for signs that she was a whore. Or perhaps they were looking for chancres. She did not know. Yue held her head high and, when she had to, greeted them politely. She had been so afraid of the other villagers knowing she had syphilis. Now that they all knew, it didn't seem such a big deal after all.

What she was most afraid of now was losing Meng Zi. He had become her religion. She had once had so many hopes. They had all been dashed, and all that remained was love. The spectre of death hovering nearby only made her feelings for him more intense. Her longing for him swamped the pain of the illness, and her fears of dying.

Every time he was due back at the village, Yue got up early and got herself ready. Then she went to wait at the turning. There was a jujube tree there and she would lean against it, her gaze fixed on the winding track along which he had to come, imagining him bouncing along on his decrepit old motorbike. The vision repeated itself a thousand times over, in her imagination. When, eventually he did appear, a small dot in the distance, her heart leapt and she felt a flood of happiness. She would set off, running to meet him and throw herself into his arms. Sometimes she actually knocked him off and they fell in the sand, laughing. Then they pulled the motorbike upright, got on together, she holding him tight around the waist, and bounced along the track towards the village.

Those were the happiest times. It was usually evening, and the great disc of the sun hung low over the sand hills. Smoke rose from village chimneys, and curled up from White Tiger Pass too. On windless days, it rose high into the air, dispersing only when it could go no higher. Then it dropped low again, forming a canopy above the villages and roads. Yue felt like she was in a fairy tale, as the motorbike put-putted along. Sometimes they met a flock of sheep returning home. The animals dawdled in front of the motorbike, oblivious to the moving wheels and, when Meng Zi beeped the horn, merely turned their stupid faces up and looked at Yue. Yue amused herself pulling faces and bleating at the sheep. There was always an answering chorus of bleats. Meng Zi laughed. 'You must have been a sheep in a former life.'

When Meng Zi had gone back to town, Yue would console herself with these memories.

Every time she passed by White Tiger Pass on her own, the pit-rats would shout after her. They were raucous, but sounded friendly. On days when Meng Zi was with her, however, they were silent, and just stared. All that she could hear then was the dull rumble of the pit machinery.

The only trouble was that time passed too slowly on days when he came back. Yue would be up and out of the door just after sunrise, but the sun was low in the evening sky before Meng Zi appeared. So Yue took buns and water and her medicine with her. 'Why are you off so early?' her mother always asked. Yue didn't explain. She just felt she couldn't stay another minute in the house. Once out of the village, there was hope. As soon as a black dot appeared far away on the winding road, she watched it intently. Sometimes, when the black dot was big enough to become a person, it turned out to be someone else. Yue did not mind. She just peered again at the end of the road.

When she left the house today, the sun had an encircling halo. That meant a sandstorm was coming. Her mother told her not to go; Meng Zi might not be able to make it. But Yue paid no attention. She wrapped her head in a headscarf and set off anyway. Her mother was right. The storm came around midday, whipping up surging waves of brown sand. The sand twisted into whirls that lashed her over and over. Leaning against the jujube tree, she was almost blown over by the wind. She squatted down and wrapped her headscarf over her nose and mouth, leaving just a slit through which she could watch the road. When the wind was at its fiercest, the road disappeared altogether into a murky cloud of wind and sand. Even the sun had disappeared. 'Don't come,' Yue muttered to herself. 'Don't come, the wind's too strong.' She was torn between fearing for his safety on the motorbike, and her desire to see him. In her emotional turmoil, she almost forgot the sandstorm.

A few villagers passed by on their way to town. When they saw a red figure sheltering against the wind, they knew it was Yue. Nowadays, they were no longer hostile, in fact some felt sorry for her. They urged her not to wait around any longer. Meng Zi would make his own way to her house if he came. Yue waited on, anyway.

Yue had lived here all her life but she had never been out in such a storm before. It was a vision of hell. Mostly, in weather like this, people stayed at home and listened to it rattling the windows, whistling in the trees, or imagined demonic voices in the strange mutterings it made. Just now, all the sounds of the storm had merged into one. Even though Yue's head was wrapped up in the scarf, sand got in through the cracks, and scoured her skin painfully.

At times, she could hardly see the road. It seemed to come and go, a streak of hazy brightness on the western horizon. The saxaul shrubs shook violently. The wind seemed to want to drag them out by their roots, but the shrubs leaned with the wind and their roots gripped the soil tightly. Peering at a shrub through her headscarf, Yue felt quite moved. That was what she needed, the tenacity of a saxaul shrub.

A black dot appeared and Yue's heart filled with happiness. Surely that must be him, mustn't it? In spite of a string of disappointments, she never lost hope that the next person would be him.

Then the dot came closer and divided into two. The couple were pushing a bike, the man in front, the woman from behind. A child was sitting on the bike seat. Their clothes were billowing in the gale. At every gust, it looked as though the bike would be blown over. When they were close enough, Yue recognized them from the village. 'Hey!' she shouted. 'Have you seen Meng Zi?' The words were snatched from her mouth by the wind. She had to repeat her question several times before they understood. 'No,' the woman said. 'We haven't seen a single person on the road. Go home. He won't come now.' Yue's face fell. Then she felt relieved. It was better for him not to attempt the trip, she thought. It was too dangerous.

As the family disappeared into the distance, Yue took refuge under the tree again, leaning her body against it so that she swayed along with its trunk. She could not help feeling that this jujube tree was her only friend in the world right now. It was strong and powerfully supple, and seemed to be protecting her. Her eyes smarted and the tears ran down her cheeks.

She did not want to go home. There was nothing comforting

about her home nowadays, it just felt oppressive. The roadside comforted her because it carried the promise of happiness. The wind howled, the sand boiled, the road appeared and disappeared, but at the end of that road there was always the possibility that the figure she longed for would appear. She would wait. Whether he came or not was almost secondary. The very process of waiting filled her heart with warmth.

The sun gradually sank towards the horizon and the wind dropped. The sand lay where it was, in its new home. Yue was sure by now that Meng Zi would not come. In such a storm, she could not blame him. Her eyes were sore with watching, but she could not tear them away from the point in the distance where the road disappeared. Finally, she saw another black dot. As it grew bigger, it looked familiar. Yue was overjoyed.

This time it was Meng Zi.

She threw herself into his arms, and he held her tight. They cried with joy and the tears washed the dust from their faces. They knew now they could never be apart.

As they passed the pit-rats, there was a cheer, as if they had been waiting for Meng Zi all day too. Yue closed her eyes and pressed her face against Meng Zi's back.

10

The sores were getting worse again. The scabbed-over ones began to weep, and ulcers appeared on her legs too. They were acutely painful. The combination of medicine from the hospital and from Old Man Liang were having no effect, and nor was the dung fire smoke treatment. A cloud of gloom descended on Yue.

Her mother found another home remedy. She had to sit in a basin filled with strong liquor. The minute the liquor touched her sores, Yue felt excruciating pain, which spread throughout her whole body. But she gritted her teeth and stuck it out. The pain made her pour with sweat but she sat there, muttering exultantly: 'Drown, you ulcers! Die from the drink!'

But bathing in liquor was no more effective than smoking her ulcers. They did not heal. Alcohol was only effective for treating external viruses. The infection was already in her blood stream, as Yue knew.

By now her father was frantic with worry. He grubbed together as much money as he could and checked her into Lanzhou City Hospital. They tried everything, except the antibiotics to which Yue was allergic. It was no use. Yue felt the spectre of death hovering behind her, leering at her.

Everything was plunged into gloom. Death had always seemed

so far away, something that happened to other people. Now it pressed in her and bared its teeth in a snarl. Yue was bewildered and afraid. Her head was a complete blank. The blankness enveloped her, cutting her off from the world. The world was outside, she was inside, her only companions helplessness and unhappiness. She lived immersed in a pain-filled nightmare, a kind of grey nothingness. If only it had been just a bad dream, she thought. Then she wrenched herself from the dream. The pain brought by the word 'death' thrust deeply into her.

Was she really going to die, she kept asking herself? She hardly seemed to have lived. Her life had flashed by. Just a few years. When she thought back on her life, it seemed as evanescent as the road in the sandstorm. A few moments stood out with great clarity: Her longing to go to school when she was little, the time she spent learning to sing the Hua'r songs, lying in Meng Zi's arms...Just those few scenes. Was that really all there was to the twenty-odd years she had lived?

Yue began to contemplate the mystery of death. Before, when someone had talked about death, it had struck Yue as depressing. Now the question of death loomed over her and there was no way she could avoid it. What happened after death, she wondered? Where would she, Yue, go to when her body was no longer alive? And so on and so forth. She could not find answers. Certainly not from her father, who avoided talking about death. But eventually these flickering thoughts and questions were extinguished by the acute feeling of despair which enveloped her.

Thank heavens, the syphilitic sores could be hidden under her clothes. There was nothing on her face to spoil her beauty. That comforted her, but saddened her too. Such a pretty face, and it was going to die.

She longed to live. She'd had such a short life. When she was little, she understood nothing. When she was a bit bigger, she was completely taken up by school homework. She'd only been able to live for herself from about age eighteen. Even then, when you took out the hours of sleep, the time she'd spent running around making a living, and times she didn't want to think about, there really wasn't much left. The only really good times in her life were those brief days with Meng Zi. It was not much of a life. If she died now, death wouldn't be much different from life.

She spent a lot of time crying.

Sometimes, she regretted not falling in love with Meng Zi earlier. When she just finished secondary school, she had a clean body then. If only they had loved, embraced, even made love, earlier. At the thought of love-making, her heart skipped a beat. How pleasurable their life together would have been. She might not-she definitely would not-have this disease. Looking back to that terrible time in the city, it was not so much that she had been deceived by someone else, it was her own emptiness that was to blame. Of course, she had hopes then too, but they had been like soap bubbles floating away from her in a dream, bursting as soon as you touched them. Every time that happened, disappointment followed. After a string of disappointments, she had felt so empty, she just wanted to steep herself in more badness. If she had not been seduced by that man, it would have been another. Empty as she was, she was unable to resist seduction. If only she had fallen in love with Meng Zi when she was younger, her life would have been so different. Every time she thought about it, she was overwhelmed with regret. Even though she knew regret was pointless, it did drown out the word 'death'. So much feeling burst from her: Pain and despair all swamped by regrets.

Should she blame fate? She'd had her fortune told a few times when she was younger and it had all been good. She was going to be a princess. She had spent her whole life waiting for her prince, which was why she hadn't chosen Meng Zi before. She'd left home, searching, searching, but had never found the man she wanted, only syphilis. She didn't understand the fortune-teller had got it so horribly wrong. Was she to blame for messing up her life, or was there some inexorable external force at work? She did not know and no one could tell her.

Lan Lan's words came into Yue's mind: 'Your heart decides your fate. A good person has a good life. A rotten person has a rotten fate.' The examples she gave all seemed to prove her point. But they didn't fit Yue. She felt she'd been too good. She had never harmed anyone. Of course, she had never gone in for good works, like Lan Lan, but there was not a scrap of malice in her. And look what a rotten fate she had. Something must have interfered with her fate, she thought, but she couldn't think what.

But one thing was absolutely clear–her desire to live, especially when she thought of Meng Zi. He had been very busy with Forestry Department work and could not make it back to the village to see her, often for days at a time. Yue found his absence unbearable. Her fierce desire to live was overtaken by an even fiercer longing to see him. When she could not bear it any more, she hitched a ride in a car going west to Liangzhou Town. Being able to see each other was a hundred times better than being stuck in that morgue-like hospital ward. She would try and persuade her dad to let her check out of hospital. When she caught up with Meng Zi, she threw her arms around him, and sank her teeth into his clothes. She dared not kiss him any more, as the doctor had told her saliva could transmit the disease. She had phoned him and asked him to get hold of some penicillin to take himself.

Very soon she was back at the hospital. The family were spending money hand over fist, buying bottle after bottle of medicine, but any antibiotics she could tolerate had no effect on the disease. Unfortunately, they were also damaging her liver, kidneys and heart. On the quiet, the doctor broke the news to her dad, who was heartbroken. Yue was beginning to smell bad, from the festering ulcers spreading down her legs. Death seemed to be inside her, emerging to grimace evilly at her. Death was like a bird with a sharp beak, and the ulcers were its beak. Yue stared at them, trying as hard as she could to keep a clear head. But bouts of confusion came more frequently, and lasted longer. She knew that death had her in its shroud, and she was like a an eagle falling into the net that could not escape, however frantically she struggled.

She hallucinated. She was trying to escape, but her feeble legs could not outrun that dark shadow. Sometimes she fell asleep and had real dreams, and in all of them she was being pursued by a great monster. As it caught her up, its shadow flowed over and pinioned her own shadow, ripping her apart, then cramming her into its gaping maw. 'Help! Meng Zi! Save me!' she cried out. Sometimes, miraculously, calling his name woke her up. Then she would be intoxicated with longing for her husband.

In her desperate state, she counted the days. She could actually feel the seconds ticking by, beating on her heart. The pain made time drag even slower. There seemed no ray of light in this dark night of the soul. At least back in the village, she had been able to go for walks along the track and wait for a dot to emerge in the far distance. Whether or not it turned out to be Meng Zi, it did at least give her hope. Now she had nothing, nothing except the pain, the doleful face of her father and the dark shadow of death.

She was going to die soon.

The odd thing was that she didn't fear dying anymore. She believed that her soul would survive. She was only afraid that it would be lonely, and selfishly hoped that Meng Zi might die with her. How wonderful to die with her beloved! At times when she was in less pain, she began to pursue this line of thought. Her most pleasurable fantasies were about Meng Zi: They were in each other's arms, they were kissing, making love, they were lying side by side on a pure white bed. They both had the disease but did not care. They just had more fun than ever. Mostly sex of course. Then one day they died, together. Their bodies died still beautiful and floated away like a pair of butterflies to the most beautiful place in the world. It had flowers, grass, pure clear water…that was as far as she got. She had a fleeting regret about never having sex with Meng Zi after they got married. It was only fleeting. The pain she was in quickly recalled her to reality. She did not have the heart to wish this pain on Meng Zi as well.

The fear that haunted her now was not dying but that, after her death, Meng Zi would marry someone else. The thought of another wedding, where she would not be the bride, was unbearable. Her death would wrench Meng Zi from her embrace and give him to another. And her soul would only be able to cry helplessly, curled up-as she imagined it-in one corner of the room, staring at the newly-married couple enjoying each other. She hated imagining that scene but, perversely, it went round and round in her head. She groaned. She really did not want to die.

Just the idea of Meng Zi remarrying inflamed her resentments, even though she knew it was irrational. She even dreamed up a couple of reasons to justify her feelings. She knew quite well that the reason Meng Zi was not with her in the hospital was because the Forestry Department wouldn't let him go, but she decided it was because he was avoiding her, that he was abandoning her. She even blamed him for the threat of divorce, which had been her mother-in-law's idea. Plus, rapid remarriage was so common in the village, sometimes when the woman's body was scarcely cold in the grave. She felt a leaden weight on her heart. Everything seemed utterly pointless. Their love would die as her body died. It all meant nothing at all: the Hua'r songs she had learnt, the money, her parents, brothers, the house, her own youth and beauty...She felt that life was one big deception, which had only become clear to her now that she was facing death.

Everything was a lie. She groaned.

Tears welled and spilled from her eyes. A sob escaped her. Her father hurried over to ask what was wrong, but she turned her head away. Grief overwhelmed her.

Now she saw everything in its true colours, she thought.

11

Meng Zi was busy doing a variety of odd jobs for the Forestry Department. He was paid 25 yuan per day, paid monthly. Today he'd had his month's wages, and put it on Yue's hospital account. He wanted more money for her but, although he asked lots of people, he couldn't get anyone to lend him any.

Then the doctors discharged Yue. The drugs were not only doing no good, they were damaging her liver and kidneys. Further in-patient treatment was just a waste of money. Her father had spent 20,000 yuan and the 10,000 Meng Zi had put on her card was gone too. Her father was all for going for more treatment, but Yue said: 'It's throwing good money after bad. I'm leaving. I don't want to stay here another day. Let me at least enjoy my last days at home.'

Back home, all the villagers dropped by. There was a great deal of sympathy for this girl, with her delicate beauty. They were moved by her faithful daily waits by the road-side. Yue was a good girl, they reckoned, always had been, good-hearted too. It was a filthy disease, true, but apart from the Buddha and the dead, was there anyone who hadn't made mistakes?

Meng Zi finally got time off work and came to visit too. Yue forgot all her resentments, and her heart leapt for joy. She was relieved to hear that he had got hold of some penicillin. Now she could stop worrying that she might have passed on the infection to him. She longed to hold him in her arms the way she had done before, to kiss him deeply, but she knew her saliva was infectious. So they could only hold hands, look at each other, weep together, laugh together. That was still good, in fact it was heaven compared to the loneliness she had suffered in her hospital bed.

Meng Zi's pay was just about enough to buy Yue the medicines she was now taking, and her belly became a laboratory for all the local herbals. They were not pleasant. She swallowed huge quantities of pills and infusions of wild herbs which had nasty side effects but were supposed to eliminate infection. She was still suffering the effects of the ox dung smoke, which had given her burns on her inner thighs, and her skin was sore from many hours' sitting in a basin. Still, every time she stepped out of doors, she took pains to dress nicely. If she did not show her legs or wear short-sleeved tops, it was because she did not want people to see her sores. She always made herself up, to cover the pallor of her face. She used moisturizing lipstick, and when no one was looking, she would check in a small hand-mirror and re-apply it. Only her parents knew how serious her illness was. To the villagers, she looked more beautiful than ever.

After all, she thought, she was still Meng Zi's wife.

Every day she tried new remedies that Lan Lan brought. She only baulked at one: swallowing live toads. She had always loathed these warty creatures. Even so, she thought she'd try it, for Meng Zi's sake, but as she raised the creature to her lips, it gave a croak. That reminded her it was alive too. Why make other creatures suffer just to lessen her own suffering? She bent down and placed it gently back in the stream. It turned and gave another little croak. Tears suddenly ran down Yue's cheeks. She almost felt as if the toad understood her.

Even the dullest people found Yue's longing for life heart-wrenching, especially when they saw her figure waiting by the roadside at the edge of the village, as she still sometimes did.

When there was no one around, Yue would kneel in the desert sands and pray to anyone and anything–the sun, Vajravarahi, and any other divinities and spirits she could think of, to vanquish the demon of her disease. If only she could be healthy for even just a few days, so that she could truly become Meng Zi's wife, just once. But it made no difference. The disease advanced inexorably. The suppurating ulcers spread all over her and soon her clothes could not conceal them.

Sometimes when no one was around to see, she and Meng Zi would weep together. As the countdown began towards the end, their love grew more passionate. But the only way they could express it was by holding hands and gazing silently into each other's eyes.

Meng Zi was still earning as much money as he could: He did odd jobs, and once or twice sneaked off to sell his blood. He never gave up searching for doctors, buying new remedies, and urging Yue to take them. She was worried because she did not want to see him get further into debt. He had borrowed from everyone he knew, but it still was not enough. Even effective painkillers were expensive. He made up his mind to borrow more money off Shuang Fu's wife when she came back to the village. He would take Yue to a hospital in Beijing. He would do whatever it took, even if he had to spend the rest of his life working like a donkey to pay it back, if only he could cure Yue.

12

One evening, the sun hung low over the sand mountains, in a murky, livid haze. Yue wanted to go to the desert, so Meng Zi borrowed a motorbike and took her. Along the narrow track where the villagers threshed the desert rice they rode, until they got to the desert. The motorbike put-puttered along, its monotonous beat like an ancient sigh. Yue sat behind side-saddle (sitting astride hurt too much), her bag over her shoulder. She was wearing clean white gloves and had put on her make-up carefully. Her face glowed. It was not far to the desert but Meng Zi deliberately went the long way round. He felt unbearably sad.

They parked the motorbike and walked up the incline together, in the light breeze. The desert had gradually been encroaching on the village and much of the land had disappeared. Many of the saxaul trees had been cut down to provide wood for the cages at the White Tiger Pass mine workings. This sand was like Yue's disease, Meng Zi thought. It would spread and gradually eat up good land. It would not be long before the whole village was swallowed up.

Meng Zi chased away some curious desert rats and sat down. Yue leaned against him. The sun bathed them in a pleasant, reviving warmth. A faint noise came to them from White Tiger Pass, unmistakably urban. Urbanization, like the sand, encroached on the village day by day. But Meng Zi knew that the sand was more powerful than the city. It could wreak havoc on it, even swallow it up so completely that it might never have existed.

Everything felt evanescent and unreal, except their embraces, under the warm sun. They lay on the sand, feeling the sweetness of being alive. Meng Zi felt that sweetness rushing away from them. He wanted to grasp it, fix it in a freeze frame, so that they could have it in in their hearts forever.

They did not talk, just as they did not think. What was the point? They just enjoyed each other's company. They would not think about the future, the future was too murky. The very act of looking forward spoiled the present. For the same reason they would not think about the past either. So they put their arms around each other, and were silent.

They did not talk about Yue's disease. They knew quite well it was devouring her. It was best not to think of it. No one was completely healthy, anyway. From the moment of birth, death started to work on everyone, with no less cruelty than syphilis. It was just that people ignored it. They went from childhood to youth, to middle age, then into old age, moving step by step, all unawares, towards the grave. In this hard-fought-for peace and quiet, they enjoyed feeling they were alive.

They became calm. They gazed out into the wilderness. Sand dunes undulated away into the unknown. Where had the dunes come from, and where did they end? They too were destructible, and would leave few traces behind when they were gone. In many years' time, there might be millions of people living here, doing the usual human things: suffering pain, uplifting their souls, yearning for a future. Would they have any idea that a man called Meng Zi and a woman called Yue had once been here? If they did not, then their lives, for which they were so grateful, were meaningless.

Meng Zi held Yue tight. She felt soft, but very real. Her breath was gentle in his ear, her heart beat so firmly, so confidently you would have said it did not know that it was disease-ridden. Her body had that special youthful suppleness. He felt it, and yet it also seemed unreal. He seemed to be moving into a world of unreality. Perhaps that was what happened with pain-the only way to bear it was to feel it as unreal. He knew of course that Yue was suffering, but he also knew quite well her pain would soon be over.

Meng Zi felt guilty. He ought to be suffering as unbearably as Yue was. But there was no way he could do that. Although from time to time, he felt pain, it was fleeting. A sense of unreality soon swept it away. All he could do was to be with her, all the time and wholeheartedly.

Yue opened her eyes and looked at the undulating sand hills. Behind her, the sun's rays shone, illuminating beads of moisture on the hairs on her face. Yue slowly turned to face him: 'Am I beautiful?' she asked quietly. Meng Zi gripped her hands. He said nothing.

Yue smiled sadly. She took her bag off the motorbike and got out a packet of incense. She lit one stick and planted it in the sand. She made Meng Zi kneel. He thought she was going to offer a prayer, but she said: 'Answer me. In the next life, will you be my husband?'

His eyes smarting, he answered: 'I'm going to marry you again in the next life.'

'Not just in the next life. For the next three lives.'

'Your next three lives.'

'No, forever.'

'Forever.'

Yue looked at him tenderly. She stroked his hair and straightened his clothes, and brushed a few specks of sand from his shoulder. Then she took his face between her hands. Looking intently at him, she said: 'Remember your vow today.' She turned her face towards the sun, which was sinking below the sand dunes on the horizon, and the dying rays made her face flame.

13

Yue was ready to die.

The ulcers had begun to spread to her neck. If she did not die soon, her beauty would die before her. She put a letter and some slippers she had embroidered under her mother's quilt. They were for Meng Zi. The envelope also held the 3,000 yuan her mother-in-law had sent her. She would not need it now. In the letter, she told her mother-in-law how grateful she was for the gift, which made her feel like she had another mother.

She applied her makeup carefully and chose her nicest outfit to wear. She put on earrings and a necklace and went to the photographic studio at White Tiger Pass to get her picture taken. She asked the photographer to give it to Meng Zi. The photographer was very taken with the results. This was her best picture, could he hang it in the window? he asked later. No, Meng Zi refused.

Before she left home, she burned everything she had used. No one interrupted her. Her mother had gone to White Tiger Pass. She was very careful. Fire was a wonderful thing, she thought. It cleansed everything, however dirty it was. She did not want to pass the infection on to anyone else.

Carrying everything she needed, she followed the road Meng Zi had taken her the other day, enjoying the walk. She had good memories of their trip together, and her face lit up in a smile. The villagers watched her from a distance. No one said anything, but Yue could feel their concern.

She left the village and walked towards the desert.

If only she could turn into a drop of cool moisture to be absorbed into its arid atmosphere.

As she looked at the undulating dunes vanishing into the unknown, it occurred to her that the same would happen to her soul. Where would she go once her soul had left her body? That was something she could not control. The only thing she could control was her remaining physical beauty. She knew she could never get her life back.

She felt there was nothing more important than beauty, especially one's beauty in the eyes of a lover. She would die now, and merge with the yellow sky and sand. Let death fix her beauty.

A great fire seemed to flicker before her eyes, fierce enough to consume all her woes. She had heard that the phoenix achieved nirvana through fire.

A soft desert breeze touched her, her only companion right now. Her cherished memories kept escaping her, like fidgety monkeys that would not keep still. Let them go, memories were unimportant.

She was in the place where she and Meng Zi had made their vow. The sand had expunged all traces of their visit but the wind still muttered the words. This made her very happy. Here she could wait for the next life to begin. Don't renege on your promise, she admonished him silently.

Yue smiled. It was an overcast day and the desert was not too hot. The sand under her was pleasantly warm. She felt, sitting down in it, as if she was in a lover's embrace. She took out her hand mirror and took one last look at herself. She could see no traces of the disease that was devouring her. She coughed. She wanted her last thoughts to be of Meng Zi, but somehow he slipped away from her. That had kept happening in the last few days. Well, that could not be helped.

Something came up and stared at Yue through round eyes. It was a lizard (or sand-baby as the villagers called them). Sand babies were children of the desert, they could put up with any amount of heat and drought. Right now, she wished she could turn into a lizard herself. Any kind of life would be better than what awaited her after death, whatever that was. She was not afraid of being reincarnated, or of hell. She was afraid of extinction…Even turning into a lizard would be better than that.

Tears ran down her face. Bitterness gnawed at her. She had not lived a happy life, ever, and she damned well resented it. That resentful anger grew and grew until it obliterated all her despair and pain. She felt a spark of life bursting from her heart.

She opened her eyes and stared back at the lizards. Their porcelain grey eyes seemed to give her strength.

When her breathing calmed down, she looked up at the sky. Its liquid azure flowed into her heart. She felt as if she had turned into the sky herself.

A long time passed.

She heard a faint sound. She thought it might be Meng Zi but when she listened carefully, she realised it was the wind.

If only I could become a phoenix! She thought.

She took deep breaths, wondering what she should do now. Eventually, it occurred to her to sing one of the Hua'r songs. Before, she had sung them for other people, but now she could sing one for herself. One should sing a song for oneself, she felt. And she pursed her lips and began in a low voice:

> *Thunder claps rumble*
> *Old men tremble*
> *Better be battered in a storm*
> *Than we two be torn asunder*

The Crunching of Broad Beans at Dead of Night

The scene that greeted Snow when she came down from the mountain was a familiar one, a recurring nightmare from which starving humans could not escape.

There had been big changes, she could see that. The gullies were littered with sinister piles of bones. A pack of wolves was gnawing at any that still had shreds of flesh on them. They stood their ground as she approached, and snarled. Snow got out her lasso, a two-pound weight tied into a nylon rope twenty feet long. She had adapted it from the weapon the villagers used to control dogs. The wolves were the dogs of the mountain god. They were afraid of ropes and when they saw the rope in her hand, their snarls turned to whimpers.

There was a smell in the air, the kind her mother used to call 'cold ash stove'. It was a smell heavy with death. There was not a spark of life, not a sign of human beings to be seen anywhere. Even the rays from the sun were wan and colourless, lacking in any vigour.

She did a quick calculation. She hadn't been in the mountains many days, but it felt like years. As if she were a Rip van Winkle.

For this trip into the mountains, grandpa Jiu had given her the Mahāmudrā (Great Seal) yoga classic, 'Following the Way of Transformation'. He had said to her: 'All phenomena are the manifestation of one's own nature, and transformation happens in one's own heart. By day you should transform your body, and by night, your dreams. Study your own nature. It belongs to the nature of emptiness, which has no nature. Everything is an illusion, and there is no place for obsession or attachment. In that way, you may enter a deeper meditative state.' Snow had followed the dharma and practiced austerity. As she walked down the mountain, she felt as if she were in a dream.

Even after she was out of the mountains, it was still a long way to Vajra Village, but all the settlements along the road seemed deserted. Everywhere were the remnants of corpses that dogs and wolves had torn apart. There was a stench in the air. The hills were full of spirits emitting vengeful, hungry wails. Snow chanted her mantras over them, but the spirits clung to the corpses lying exposed in the wilderness. There was nothing she could do to help the dead. Fine, she thought, if you want to stand guard over the souls of the dead, you go ahead.

Then she saw someone peeling the fine bark off an elm. On the main trunk, the bark had almost been stripped bare, leaving the white pith exposed. Only the branches still had bark on, and this he was scraping carefully into a dish. He looked terribly emaciated, and trembled so badly that he surely could not last much longer. Snow cut off a piece of wolf meat and gave it to him. His eyes glistened with joy, he grabbed the meat and sank his teeth into it. He shook it violently from side to side, like a wild dog wrestling with the flesh of an ox.

'What's happened to you?' asked Snow.

The man ignored her, giving all his attention to chewing. Finally, he said: 'Dead, dead, almost all dead and gone.' What's happened at Vajra Village?' asked Snow. 'I don't know. I've heard they're all right, but people have gone in and no one's come out of there. I've heard that the people who went in were cooked and eaten.' 'What nonsense,' said Snow, dismissively. 'Vajra Village people aren't cannibals.'

She gave a long sigh. She knew that the desolation she had passed on the way was bound to be just as bad at Vajra Village.

At noon, she was finally within sight of Vajra Village. As she drew nearer, she saw some people's militiamen beating someone up. The man was wailing: 'I was only running away to survive! What's wrong with that?' 'Oh no, you don't!' they said. 'If we're going to die, we'll die together.' And they dragged him back into the village.

Snow took a side street and walked up House Screen Hill. From her vantage point, the deserted village was just as desolate as she had guessed. The gully was full of stinking corpses. The north-facing hillside swarmed with black dots, either wolves or wild dogs.

She followed the crest of the hill down. Her uncle's house stood at the foot of the mountain, so far from the other houses that they hardly ever had visitors. Her impression of her uncle was that he was dishonest and heartless. Although he was supposed to be a well-educated man, he was actually as quarrelsome as a fighting cock. There was a time when he used to come to Snow's house when there was not enough to eat at home. He loved vinegar-sauced yam noodles. Her mother would let the noodles cool and dress them in vinegar sauce. Her uncle would slurp them down. But then he would put down his chopsticks and curse his sister in front of all the villagers, accusing her of letting the side down and giving the family a bad reputation. Her mother always humoured him, because he was all the family she had, and blood was thicker than water. When she, Snow, got angry with her uncle, her mother told her that he was head of the family on her side, and without him, where would Snow be? Actually, her uncle spoilt his niece and used to promise her all sorts of treats.

The stench was getting worse, and Snow held her nose as she walked. She could not help remembering everything the villagers had done wrong. She wanted nothing to do with them, didn't even want to think about them. Grandpa Jiu used to say she should try to be more compassionate. But in her daily devotions, even though she offered up prayers for all living things, these villagers didn't seem to feature among them. She felt only anger towards these people who had put her mother through such torment. Get rid of your anger, Grandpa Jiu used to tell her. Remember, rage leads to hell.

The gate to her uncle's smallholding was shut tight. Snow did not need to knock. She slipped the latch and went in. San zhuan was sunning himself in the courtyard and greeted her with a smile. His flesh hung loose on him, but his smile was still brilliant. 'Mum!' he shouted joyfully. 'Cousin's here!' In a little while, her aunt came out of the house. Her face was so swollen that her eyes were just narrow slits. She greeted Snow with a grunt and invited her indoors. The house was covered in several days' worth of dust. Her uncle had been lying on the *kang* bed but struggled to raise himself when he saw her. He didn't ask her anything, although his silence spoke volumes. She wondered if the trouble she had got into had

had repercussions for her uncle. He might have been educated, but he was poor, and no one in the village respected him. Her aunt, if the rumours were true, would drop her trousers for any man in the village, and when the village men had nothing better to do, they would talk about her amours at the corner of the south wall. She was said to beat her skinny runt of a husband, push him to the ground and sit on him with her big heavy arse until he howled in agony. She had her good points though. She was a ferociously hard worker. At harvest time, everyone was told if they cut one *mu* of grain, they'd get paid for three days' work. But her aunt could scythe from the afternoon right through until the next morning. She could cut one and a half *mu* of wheat in twenty-four hours, which meant she earned four and a half days' wages in a day's work. She was the biggest earner in the whole village, and when the wages were calculated each autumn, her uncle brought home enough wheat to keep them going for at least six months.

Uncle dragged himself upright, still saying nothing. Snow thought this was for the best, as she did not want to tell him where she had been. She got out the wolf meat and the three children threw themselves at her. Auntie slapped them away, and they howled in protest. But they were so weak with hunger that the wails came out as faint gasps. They're really starving, thought Snow, and she cut some slices of wolf meat and divided it between them. San zhuan swallowed his own portion, grabbed his elder brother's piece and rushed away. The older boy bawled and Snow gave him another bit.

'You're a disgrace!' shouted auntie.

Snow said nothing. She did not like her aunt, in fact she was disgusted not just by her swollen face, but by her behaviour when her uncle was away from home: She brought lovers into the house. Once, at New Year, Snow's mother made her go and see her uncle, and Snow found her aunt too busy fooling around and bantering with a bunch of men sitting on the *kang* bed to pay any attention to Snow. After that, Snow hardly ever went there again.

'Why have so many people died in the village?' Snow asked her uncle. 'Is the granary really empty?'

'They're keeping the grain for war-time,' said her uncle. 'And it's being watched. People have died in almost every family in the village. A lot of families have had every member die. If it goes on like this, the village will be gone completely.' 'If we're going to die, we might as well all die together,' said her aunt. Her eyes gleamed with hatred, and Snow shivered. Her aunt had changed. She had never had any morals, true, but the menacing air about her was new. Hatred changes people, she felt.

Snow gave her uncle a piece of meat, and he gobbled it up. His eyes were glazed, and sunk deep in their sockets. 'This is the end,' he said. 'We won't last till winter.'

'The wheat's not ready to harvest yet,' said Snow, 'but there are ears on it. We can steal some to eat.' 'Don't talk nonsense,' her aunt said, looking around in alarm. 'You could get beaten to death for it. Some of the corpses in the gully starved to death, but some got beaten to death.'

'Get some water, girl,' said her uncle. 'We can't eat the meat unless you cook it a bit.' Snow went outside for some straw, then took the lid off the cooking pot, and discovered there was something in it covered in green hairs. A familiar stink rushed up her nose. Her aunt gave her a sideways glance. Snow got the ladle and scraped the hairs off. Underneath, she found that the smell came from some bits of meat. Where had they got the meat from, she wondered? It was mutton a monk had brought, her uncle explained. Snow stifled her disgust and shovelled the stinking, sticky mess into a washbowl. Suddenly, she uncovered something that looked like a finger.

Auntie giggled. 'You got to be canny to survive,' she said.

Snow suppressed her disgust, washed the pot out, added water and boiled the wolf meat. She felt her aunt's eyes raking her hungrily and dared not look round. She went to get more straw. The children were watching the pot from a distance. They're children, she thought. With a bit of food in their bellies, they'll soon brighten up. Suddenly, she caught a glance from San zhuan which was exactly like his mother's expression. It silenced her.

Smoke from the stovepipe rose into the sky, hung there, then settled, misting up the courtyard. The smoke too had a conspiratorial smell, she felt, as if it was coiling around her. Things seemed ever more dreamlike.

With the bundle of wheat straw in her arms, Snow went back into the house. Her uncle asked how she was getting on. He meant her mother. He never called her sister, just 'she'. Snow grunted. She stuffed the straw into the stove and the steam rose from the pot. Heat radiated from the fire. The firelight made Snow smile...she really was over-reacting. Now she only saw excitement in her aunt's eyes, although the woman said nothing. She was a strong-minded woman. Of course, she would not want Snow to see her family in such distress. Snow wanted to say that everyone was in the same boat these days, but she knew that would embarrass her aunt. Better to keep quiet.

When the wolf meat had cooked for a while, Snow poked it with the chopsticks. It was tender. She tore it into long shreds, added more water, and asked where the salt was. 'We haven't tasted salt for more than six months' was her aunt's reply. Snow ladled out a bowl for her uncle, because she saw the shadow of her mother's face in his. She felt a rush of affection. She picked out some pieces of meat and served them to him. She heard a slurping, her aunt drinking some broth from the ladle. The children rushed at her, and her aunt pushed them away so hard they tumbled out of the door. But they did not cry. They just crawled to their feet and stared at their parents' mouths. Snow felt her eyes smart with tears.

When the adults had had half a bowl each, Snow said they should not drink any more in case they swelled up. She took the bowl and called the children. They ran to her and she fed them a spoonful each at a time. She should have brought more wolf meat, she thought.

'Don't go,' said her aunt. 'Now it's night, there's something I want to tell you.'

Snow looked at the dust-covered *kang* bed, and frowned. 'Mum will be worried,' she said. In fact, when she had set off, her mother had told her to stay overnight if it was late, and on no account to walk home in the dark. Snow didn't want to walk home in the dark either. Her skin crawled at the thought of the corpses along the way, but she was afraid of the *kang* bed in her uncle's house too.

'Stay,' urged her uncle. 'If you stay the night, I'll tell you about your mum. I'm not long for this world.'

Fine, thought Snow, I'll stick it for a night.

The wan moonlight crept in through the plastic-covered windows and shone on the heads crowded on the *kang* bed.

Her auntie had gone to sleep in the inner room with San zhuan.

The *kang* bed in there was covered in wheat straw, so that was their mattress. Snow felt bad for them.

Her uncle's voice was hollow, as if he were sleep-talking. He began to tell her mother's story. Some of it Snow had already heard, for instance, her mother had told her that so many people had died that their heads littered the river shore like boulders. Her mum had told her how the cavalry, who so enjoyed beheading people, had spurred their horses and thundered down on them, and she had run and run, hearing the pattering of hooves coming after her like fine rain. Heads flew, spinning through the air and landing with horrible thuds. Their mouths agape, they looked as if they wanted to bite the knife-wielders but only ended up with a mouthful of sand and grit. Then they were tied on the horses' rumps as a trophy.

'Your mother ran and ran,' said uncle, 'but she couldn't outrun these ghouls. The knives swished and the heads of the men alongside her flew. The women were chased into a compound. One pursuer became your mother's husband.'

'And that was how your mother was taken captive,' her uncle sighed.

Her mother never talked about what happened to her next.

The villagers all knew though.

Snow did not want to re-open old wounds.

'That's enough of that,' said her uncle, and silence fell.

The wan moonlight crept in through the plastic-covered windows and shone on the heads crowded on the *kang* bed.

Snow felt as if she was in a dream.

The sound of crunching on broad beans came from the inner room. It was a scary sound at dead of night. Snow was not sleepy. Her uncle's words echoed in her head. The moonlight shone on her uncle's face and his lips nibbled furiously, as though he was eating the rays. The glow, bathing his features, made him look happy, but his munching lips sounded very odd. The children had gone asleep, but Snow still had the feeling they were watching her through half-open lids. From a distance came the yapping and barking of squabbling wolves and wild dogs. They were making a lot of noise.

Her aunt was still crunching the beans. Wherever had she got them from, wondered Snow? She hadn't eaten beans in an age. The last time, she remembered, was when the clan distributed bonuses and she got some dried-fried beans. She remembered how delicious they were. The sound of her aunt crunching them made her mouth water.

She's so greedy, she thought. She hasn't even shared them with uncle.

Suddenly she heard a cry from the other room: 'Snow! Snow!' Snow did not want her aunt to know that she had been listening, and did not answer.

Then she heard a rustling, and the sound of footsteps. Snow was curious enough to half-open her eyes. In the moonlight, she thought she saw her auntie put a finger in her mouth. Snow felt her heart miss a beat. Then her aunt tiptoed over to the sleeping children, opened her mouth and blew a long, slow breath in their faces. Snow knew what that was: It was called 'spurting energy'. When the village children were too ill to eat, their mothers waited until they were asleep and did it to them, to pass some of their own energy to the sick children. People used it when they were trapped in the desert too; if two were together, they would breathe into each other's mouths. Doing that could keep them alive for a long time. So she really was a devoted mother after all, thought Snow.

Auntie breathed on her children some more, went back into her room, then came straight out again. In the moonlight, her face looked pale and strained, though it was less swollen. She was a good-looking woman, thought Snow. No wonder the village men were so keen on her. She was startled at the dark look her aunt gave her. The woman had a pestle for smashing ginger in her hand. The pestle had a pointed end and it gleamed blue like a will'o'the'wisp. Snow knew all about them. She had seen the way they licked the sky like feathered serpents. Her aunt moved slowly and silently across the room towards the *kang* bed. Her uncle's lips were still now, as if he had had enough moonlight to eat. Its rays still stole through the window, as if bringing bad news. Her aunt's eyes gleamed blue too. Snow was afraid of that gleam, though not of her aunt. She pulled herself together. She moved her fingers a little, and found she could move them quite easily. She was reassured.

Her aunt's figure threw an enormous shadow. It was an illusion, of course. If Snow stood up, she knew her aunt would appear a normal size. She wondered what the woman was doing. Now the answer was becoming clear. She saw hesitation on her aunt's face, and an inner struggle. She knew her aunt did not like her, but she had brought wolf meat for them, after all. Her uncle turned over and she knew he was awake. She heard him whisper: 'What the hell are you doing?' There was no reply. Snow wished he had not woken up. Because he had woken up, she had lost her uncle forever. She heard him say he didn't want her to suffer. Well, at least he remembered she was his niece, Snow thought. She wondered why it had not occurred to them that she might be awake. She suddenly felt a rope around her neck. The children held one end, her uncle the other. They were holding their breath, ready to pull hard if she woke up. If the three children were involved, there was no hope for her. She realised that her aunt had been breathing into their mouths to wake them up.

Her aunt raised the pestle high above her head, so she could strike as hard as possible. Her eyes were big and round. Snow remembered how they had been like slits. In the darkness, everyone's faces seemed unfamiliar, as if they were sneering at her. Snow realised why other families had lost so many children, but her uncle and aunt, only one. It dawned on her that her aunt's lovers were all dead men. The pestle had killed them all, she realised. She had lured them into bed, then dispatched them with a blow of the pestle. They were all ghosts now, and she seemed to see them peering at her, just waiting to take over her body when she died, or violate her when she joined them in the underworld. The room filled with people suddenly, all armed with pestles. She was surrounded.

The pestle came down with a rush of air. Then it slowed, was suspended in mid-air. The men were all cheering it on, their teeth bared, their breath foul, blood-shot eyes glaring. They knew Snow was awake, and were making sure her aunt knew it too. Her aunt took no notice. Snow could have reached out and grasped her wrist. With a quick twist, she could have broken it. She imagined it snapping like firewood, the sound loud in the quiet room. The rope lay coiled on her neck, poised like a snake ready to strike. Snow felt a quiver of excitement run through the rope. They salivated for her young girl's flesh. They had had enough of the coarse flesh of old men. They did not care that she was a cousin or a niece, to them she was a morsel of meat, from her tender breasts to the firm pads of her palms. Her muscles were as appetising as butter and as for her tongue. …Snow could almost see their mouths, dripping with oil, taking a bite of her flesh, and hear her aunt crunching on her finger, the way she had crunched on the broad beans. Her aunt looked so beautiful, her lips sensual as they nibbled. The attendant ghouls, fluttering and dancing around her, drooled at the sight.

The pestles continued to drop slowly, dragging through the air. Blue light darted everywhere, like swarms of rats grinding their teeth. As the pestle appeared about to kiss the top of Snow's head, she heard her aunt mutter: 'Die! Die!' her aunt was waiting for the sound of the impact. Just what kind of sound-dull or sharp, loud or quiet, high-pitched or low-depended on what the pestle was meeting. A splat, and you knew that the pestle had thumped a fat man, or a nose, splattering mucus in all directions. Disgusting. A crisp, cheerful sound and it was a skinny person, or a forehead. A hard blow to the forehead, and the brain matter spurted out, and would be wasted. Brains were the most nourishing part of the body. That, and the eyeballs, were the bits San zhuan liked best. Whenever the steam rushed up from the pot, he got there first, and stuck his finger and thumb in, and pulled out the eyeball and the flesh that clung to it. The eyeballs were black, but the surrounding matter was greyish white. Delicious when you sank your teeth into it. So delicious that it even chased away the bitterness in brackish water. Her aunt was hoping for a sharp sound like this, because her old man had told her not to let the girl suffer. And she was a kind-hearted woman, she didn't want to hurt her niece either; she hoped that the pestle would strike home to the temple, and the blow would knock the girl out and kill her. She was like an executioner, she knew all the tricks of the trade. She wanted to hear a clear, sharp sound.

To her surprise, what she heard was a dull thud, as if she had pounded the pestle into someone's belly. Auntie was shocked to see that Snow was watching her. She did not know where the pestle had landed but thought it must be on the pillow, though that was under Snow's head.

Auntie cried out, not caring whom she woke up. She whirled the pestle madly, but every time it seemed to land on the pillow, even though the latter was obviously tucked underneath Snow's head.

Auntie finally ran out of steam.

She threw down the pestle, went into the kitchen and rushed out again with a knife. 'What are you waiting for?' she cried. 'Do you think you'll live if you let her go?' She was not just talking about her next meal, but about stopping the girl from blabbing.

There was a swish of the knife. It was hard to believe that her aunt, weakened by hunger, could handle it so. After all, all her practice had come from making dumplings. Yet, strangely, the sword still landed on the pillow. Straw from the pillow flew in all directions, like dragonflies filling the room.

'Pull the rope tight!' cried her aunt.

Snow felt the rope tighten around her neck. Afraid they might pin her down, she gave it a swift tug, and went out into the courtyard. She left her aunt behind, still slashing the pillow.

Her uncle and the children hung on and were in the courtyard with her. Snow had had enough of them. She threw off the rope and the children flew in all directions like shooting stars. Not very heavy, thought Snow. They really are starving.

Auntie flung down the knife and wailed: 'We want to live too, girl!'

Snow's uncle and the children let go of her, and scattered like black birds.

The children cried too. A black shadow knelt before Snow. It was uncle.

Uncle burst into torrents of tears.

The Women, the Camels and the Dholes

Ying and Lan Lan were not expecting to meet dholes so soon after they got to the desert.

Dholes, a kind of wild dog, were the creatures the herders most feared. They were especially adept at disemboweling cattle and would even do the same sometimes on camels. That was quite a feat, because the dhole had to jump high enough to sink its teeth into the camels' gut. If it didn't succeed, the camel would raise one back leg and like Ronaldo taking a penalty kick, hurl the dhole high into the air.

Don't go worrying yourself about dholes as they have a native skill at springing vertically into the air, just like you're good at nodding off when you read a novel. These intelligent dholes are quicker off the mark than any footballer. Of course if the camel is nimble enough, it can try out its kicks on dholes who are old or sick.

One thing is certain: The dhole is no footballer itself.

If you want to know why the dholes are so feared, you can go and interview an animal they've disembowelled. But you won't find any. There are no disembowelled animals left alive to tell the tale. They've all been long since consigned to the underworld. So to the underworld you must go, if you want that interview. But, as our respected forebears said, animals never stay there longer than 49 days. Afterwards, dumb animals that they are, they'll find a new home. Even if they are eager to be interviewed by you, their bodies are not under their control. Animals lack mindfulness. Their karma will allocate them some appropriate, new destination, despite themselves.

Dholes are small animals, no bigger than raccoons. Of course, this is a meaningless comparison for most people nowadays, who won't have seen a raccoon. So let's say that dholes are the size of a small fox. You'll know, of course, that foxes are smaller than elephants, but just how much smaller you'd probably be hard put to say. So here's my last shot: If your wife is a slender woman, a dhole is no bigger than her calf muscles.

Get it?

So, an animal about the size of the calf muscles of your lovely wife can make the herders quake with fear. Of course there's a good reason for that. It's nothing to do with the animal's shape, just the same way as people arouse fear in others irrespective of their size.

But I'm getting off the point.

In what way are dholes so frightening? My readers will want to ask. I don't really have the credentials to answer that question, because I've never been to the underworld to interview a dhole's victim, nor have I ever fallen victim, to the beast myself.

Anyway, I'll begin by taking an example from the criminal law: Suppose that I'm a hanging judge. I have you tied to a bench in front of me. It doesn't matter whether you're tied face up or face down. All I'm concerned about is that there's a bamboo growing nearby, with plenty of whippy stems. Then I open you up and scoop out your intestines. Then I bend down a three-metre tall bamboo cane, and attach it to your guts—and I let go. What happens? Right, the cane springs back upright, pulling all the intestines out with it, ripping them away from your anus.

Now you'll have a better idea why dholes are so frightening.

So many of the pack animals killed by dholes end their lives that way. The dhole springs up and sinks its teeth into its belly, and then drops and dashes away. The guts in its mouth are accompanied by great spurts of blood, of course. I can't tell you whether this causes the animal to shriek in pain, because I haven't been there, but I've seen the herders who were, and I can tell you they always go pale at the memory. In fact, they can't even tell you how scared they were, *they just gurgle wordlessly.*

I remember the first time I heard about dholes, it gave me a pain in the arse for days after. I actually dreamed that the dholes were ripping out my guts.

So why, you might well ask, did those two young women go to a place where there were dholes?

Very good question.

It was actually very simple. Each of them had been thwarted in her desires. But they didn't want to accept that. Simple, no? Everything in this world is very simple really. Even world wars boil down to one bunch of people fighting another bunch of people. But what appears to be so straightforward actually turns out to be a whole lot more complicated than you think.

And that's exactly what the story follows is about.

1

Sometime during the day, the women saw a lot of faint dots on a distant sand dune. Some of them were advancing on the wild camel carcass they had passed, others stayed put. Ying knew at once they were dholes and her mouth went dry with fear. She looked beseechingly at Lan Lan. Lan Lan went for a closer look, holding her gun in both hands, and came back saying comfortingly: 'Don't worry, they're only moving in to feed. The camel is big enough to feed them all. They won't risk attacking humans.' Ying wanted to say: 'Maybe it's us they're after.' She was numb with fear and her legs almost gave way under her.

The camels gazed at the distant dune, as if alert to the danger. They made honking noises. They sensed the threat, Ying knew that. She had heard that dholes weren't afraid of camels spitting, though wolves were. Ying's bull camel snorted again and looked round at Ying as if to say: 'Don't be afraid, I'm here.' She was touched. Camels weren't often so caring. In fact, most people weren't. It was all too common in this world for people to hit someone who was down, fleece them mercilessly, and stand by while they were attacked. Real solidarity was rare, even though sometimes all it took was a few words of comfort to rescue someone who was close to despair.

And she was comforted. At least if she died at the hands of the dholes today, she wouldn't die alone. The thought stopped her feeling afraid. 'You don't be afraid either,' she said to Lan Lan. 'Even if they rush us, we'll be fine. Losing a head only leaves a scar the size of a bowl.' Lan Lan smiled and put her gun down. 'Right,' she said. 'There's absolutely nothing to be afraid of. What's so great about living anyway? The only thing I'm not too happy about is being swallowed up by a pack of dholes.'

'Honestly,' said Ying, 'It doesn't matter who swallows you. You may see the dholes as evil, but the pups think their parents are wonderful. Forget them, if we're going to die, at least we won't die hungry.' And she poured some water into the pan, lit the fire, and began to mix in the flour.

Lan Lan cheered up and started chopping brushwood for fuel. The sounds of her chopping reached the dholes and caused a commotion in the pack. Maybe they were afraid of humans too, thought Ying.

When they had eaten, Lan Lan built the fire up again. She chopped enough fuel to keep it going all night. They didn't put up their tent, just rolled out their bedding next to the fire. Because of the dholes, Lan Lan wouldn't let the camels wander off to graze the scrub. Instead, she made them lie down around the bonfire, facing outwards. That way, if the dholes were really intent on ripping out their guts, they would have to come close to the fire. The camels did as they were told, as if they understood. Ying brought them armfuls of twigs to eat.

Lan Lan laid out the skin from the wild camel, fur upwards, so that the sand would absorb some of the moisture during the night, and make the skin lighter. When they got to the saltpans, they could rub salt in, to stop the moths or bugs spoiling it.

Not long after dark, they heard the sound of tearing flesh from where the carcass lay. The muffled angry growling from the dholes carried far in the night air. Wave after wave of terrifying sounds reached them. The camels flattened their ears and snorted again. Camels, normally the most unflappable of beasts, rarely flattened their ears like this. It showed they were truly frightened of the creatures. As for Ying, although she had said she wasn't frightened of dying, thinking of the dholes made her quake all over.

The sound of tearing flesh grew more fearsome. The dholes must be fighting fiercely over the flesh, it can't be enough to fill their bellies, Ying thought, very afraid. She knew that if the dholes gorged until they were full, then she and Lan Lan were relatively safe. But if they were still hungry when they had consumed the camel, they would come after the girls and their live camels. Suddenly Ying thought of her home village and her mum. It was a distant, fuzzy memory. The village seemed like another world. She saw her mother's gentle smile. It occurred to Ying that if she had had any idea of what was to happen, she would never have rowed with her mother. But the thought also reminded her that her mother had been planning to marry her to the slaughterman, and that she refused to do. I'll wait for you, Ling Guan, my love, she thought. One day we'll be reunited. And when I've earned enough money, my older brother can get married again and mum won't push me any more.

Lan Lan took the bag of gunpowder and shot and put it down further from the flames. Ying was feeding the fire with twigs, a few at a time. She knew that wolves were afraid of fire, but she didn't know about dholes. If they weren't, then the girls stood little chance. If the pack of dholes charged them, even machine guns wouldn't stop them, let alone a rather small firearm.

The growling and yapping over the dead camel grew in volume until it sounded like a fierce battle. There were blood-curdling screeches, bellows, growls and yelps, interspersed with wolf-like howls. Ying's scalp crawled. 'Dholes and wolves fight over food,' said Lan Lan. 'There are so many dholes there, they could eat a wolf.'

Louder and louder rose the cacophony, exploding outwards until it seemed to make the stars quiver and fade. A great tornado of sound ricocheted through the gully. Suddenly they heard a dull ripping and the howls became intermittent and were finally drowned out altogether. Then there were more howls and something tore away into the distance. In her mind's eye, Ying saw the dholes, their fangs bared in a malicious grin, racing in pursuit.

Lan Lan squeezed Ying's hand. Ying smiled and gave an answering squeeze. Their palms were moist with sweat. 'What are we going to do?' asked Ying quietly. 'Should we leave?' 'It's too late for that,' said Lan Lan. 'We can never outrun the dholes. Let's gather more brushwood. We'll have to stick it out until daylight...'

She gave Ying the torch and took the machete for herself. 'We'll cut all the scrub we can find in the gully, even if it's wet.'

Now that the dholes were eating, the camels had settled down again. The feeding frenzy grew fiercer. Dholes did not have any fixed place to feed. They went wherever the herds were. They had no lairs either, unless it was the mating season, when the female dholes would drag their heavy bellies to some place where they could give birth and nurture their pups for a few months. Once the pups were grown, dholes went back to being the tornadoes of the desert, plundering food wherever they could. They were not territorial. Unlike wolves and jackals, they did not mark their domains with urine. And because they had no territory, everywhere was their territory. Anywhere there was life, they roared in and ripped into anything they wanted to eat. To desert travellers, they were a menace.

Lan Lan was focused on keeping the fire low but still just alight. The fire and her gun were the only two things in the world she could rely on. When they got ready for the fine-sand desert, her father had put petrol and gas lighters in their bags, as well as firewood. In the desert, if you had fire, you could keep going. Now she understood why he had spread those items around their bags when he packed them. He was afraid the women might lose the lighters or use them up. She smiled to herself at his foolishness.

Lan Lan put the packsaddles down close by the fire. The gunpowder she put a little further away. She spread the smelly, just-flayed camel skin on the sand nearby. Every now and then they got a whiff of it. If they hadn't stopped to skin the dead camel, they would have been miles away by now. By stopping, they had taken the gamble, without knowing if it would pay off or not. There was no point brooding on it. What was done was done. If disaster really did strike, there would be no escaping it. They were so far away from anywhere, they might even meet up with a pack of wolves.

Lan Lan put the gun a bit further away from the flames, in case a spark ignited the powder. She told Ying to take a nap. The dholes wouldn't bother them now. If they didn't get enough from the carcass, then it might occur to them to attack the humans. If that happened, there wouldn't be time to sleep. 'You sleep a bit,' said Ying. 'You did all the work flaying the camel carcass. You must be exhausted.' 'All right,' said Lan Lan, 'Just don't let the fire go out, and don't use up all the brushwood. The gun's loaded, so be careful.' Then she propped herself against the pack saddles and soon Ying could hear faint snoring. She's a brave woman, thought Ying, to be able to sleep soundly in circumstances like this. She was right, though, if you weren't afraid of dying, what else was there to worry about? All the same, Ying really didn't fancy the idea of dying in the jaws of a dhole.

Ying added a bit more brushwood and the flames leapt up. She felt drained of energy, as if she was hundreds of years old. Even if they died tonight, she wouldn't be cut off in her prime, at least, that was how she felt. She sometimes thought that people were born simply to suffer, and since everyone was going to die sooner or later, it was really no different from never having been born. So why bother? She smiled sadly to herself.

The rending and tearing noises had subsided, although every now and then she heard them. There must still be flesh on the carcass for the dholes to eat. That should have given her time to think about herself, but she could no longer be bothered. It was so pointless. It wasn't as if you could change your fate by thinking. Sometimes thinking just made things feel worse.

Sometimes, though, it was important to think. For instance, just now, she wanted to conjure up Ling Guan. The memory was seductive, and she felt herself grow hot down there. It was only thoughts like that that had driven her to action. Without them, she would not have done anything, and the story of her life would have been very different. It seemed that your fate often depended on what thoughts went through your head. It occurred to her that there were widows in the village who, when their husbands were scarcely cold in the grave, found themselves another man to smile at. Those were the thoughts that went through their heads, and drove them to act as they did. And those actions, in turn, determined their fate.

No more thinking. She poked and puffed at the fire, making the flames lick at the damp twigs. She loved the hissing that came from burning damp twigs. Together with birdsong, it was some of the most beautiful music in nature. She might have thought of the sounds of tearing flesh as music too, if only the dholes had not been a threat. She listened carefully. There were gentler sounds beneath the savage growling, maybe the mother dhole feeding her pups. The thought brought her son Pan Pan and his sweet baby face to her mind. A tide of emotion swept over her. She longed to fly back home to give him fierce nibbles.

The rending and ripping sounds gradually faded.

A great silence enveloped them. Ying felt as if she could see green eyes shining through the darkness. She had never had the chance to examine dhole eyes close-up, but she had seen the eyes of mad dogs in the village. Presumably dholes looked at humans the same way, except that dholes had green eyes and mad dogs' eyes were red. The colour was neither here nor there, they were all greedy and all savage. She knew what greed looked like. It was the expression Poxy Xu the matchmaker had when he looked at her. The very thought made her retch, and she shook her head fiercely to get rid of it. What did savagery look like in someone's eyes? She couldn't imagine. She remembered the fierce resentment in her mother's eyes sometimes when she looked at her, but was it fair to use the word 'savagery'? Apart from that, she could think of no other instances of savagery that she had come across. Instead, she saw a combination of Poxy Xu and the mad dogs in the dholes' eyes that peered at her out of the night.

Ying retched again. She preferred to be surrounded by the eyes of mad dogs than have to see Poxy Xu again.

Suddenly, the camels spat. Ying was startled. It was a sign that they sensed danger nearby. She prodded Lan Lan and put the torch on. The beam played over the distant dunes, which was now densely covered with green lights. They shone brilliantly, and moved back and forth like phosphorescence. Ying shivered. She threw a stick in the direction of the lights and puffed hard, making the lights prance around. 'Don't be afraid,' said Lan Lan in a low voice. 'They're afraid of fire.' She fetched the gun and held it with the barrel pointing skyward. 'Why not fire a shot to scare them off?' said Ying. 'There's nothing to worry about yet,' said Lan Lan. 'If they don't come any closer, then we can just ignore them. At the moment, we're all in the same boat. They're scared of us and we're scared of them. If I fire and they get used to the sound of gunfire, then we're really in trouble.' She got out the tilley lamp and lit it.

To make it harder for the dholes to sneak up on them, Lan Lan moved the bedding and the packsaddles so that they had their backs to the camels, instead of facing the camels, like before. Camels have night sight. This way, they had more eyes to keep watch. They didn't need to watch their backs, just what was in front of them.

Lan Lan was beginning to feel sorry that she hadn't cut more brushwood. She had never been in this situation before and she didn't know how big a fire was needed to keep the dholes at bay. Obviously if they began to creep closer, then they needed a bigger fire and, in that case, their fuel wouldn't last until daylight.

Ying felt terror creeping over her.

2

Dholes had fallen completely silent. They must be sizing up the opposition. They could take their time. The carcass had taken the edge off their hunger. The camels had stopped chewing and were not spitting either. The only sound to be heard was the hissing of the flames. Ying began to feel oppressed by the silence. It was an odd feeling. She had always liked silence and hated noise and bustle. She had never imagined that silence could be such an assault on her senses. Her heart began to thud in her chest. The gully in the dunes where they were camped swelled with heartbeats. She could hear Lan Lan's, the camels' and the dholes' too. Lan Lan's heart thudded, the camels' sounded like a stone roller slowly turning, and the dholes' pitter-pattered, like stones heated in a pot. The pitter-pattering grew louder and the sound set her teeth on edge, grating like countless saw blades being drawn back and forth. She shook her head and forced herself to steady her breathing. But she could still hear the sound, as if the dholes were grinding their teeth. Lan Lan's Dad had said that he had seen a million rats grinding their teeth, with his own eyes, and the noise could reduce a human to a quivering wreck. Ying reckoned the sound of dholes grinding their teeth was worse than rats. And, strangely, the sound of her own heart thudding grew louder too. She hoped her heart could stand the strain.

Lan Lan threw a few sticks on the fire and the flames leapt up a little higher. But they only cast a light for a distance of ten or so metres. The flames seemed to smudge the outline of the far-off dunes. If the dholes crept silently forward and rushed them, thought Ying, there was nothing they could do. She turned on the torch again. Its powerful beam made the dark shapes leap wildly, almost as they took the torch for a bolt of lightning. She had heard that all animals were afraid of thunderstorms, with good reason: The desert was littered with the corpses of animals that had been struck by lightning. Never mind ordinary animals, even the canniest of elves, moon-worshippers, lickers of a girl's first bleeding, suckers of the vital essence of young boys, creatures who could live a thousand years, were afraid of lightning. They knew it could reduce them to a pile of ashes. Of course, the dholes were afraid of a torch beam that looked like a bolt of lighting.

Ying found their panic reassuring. Just so long as you're afraid of something, she thought. So the torch was one more thing, besides fire and guns, that would keep them at bay. The torch had four batteries in it and they had eight spares, so even if they used it continuously, it would last for several hours.

As soon as she switched it off, she was blind again. Only the vague outline of the dunes was visible. Paradoxically, it was only when the fire was low that they could see the green orbs shining in the darkness. They were afraid to let it burn too low in case the dholes attacked. But if they made the fire bigger, then it blinded them. It was as if they and the camels were on stage and the dholes were the audience. The watchers' gaze was focused on them, but they could see almost nothing themselves. It was frightening.

Lan Lan had an idea: She left Ying in charge of the fire and she took the gun, the powder and the torch and found a hiding place a little distance away. That way, she could see better. If the dholes rushed her, she could turn the gun on them.

Lan Lan soon realised she was surrounded by swiftly moving green orbs. Obviously the greedy animals were coming closer. She took aim at the densest cluster of orbs, pressed the trigger and there was a spurt of gunfire. She heard a chorus of yelps and the orbs retreated. Lan Lan smiled in satisfaction. That would show them who was boss. Did they think that all she was carrying was a firelighter?

The gunfire at least had the effect of making the blobs visible in the torch beam smaller. They now looked as though they were 100 metres away, at least. The gun held a good number of pellets but the range was twenty or thirty metres, no more. She had hit a few of them, but probably only scratched them. Lan Lan loaded the gun with a ball-bearing. That way, she could fire further. A ball-bearing could bring down a Mongolian gazelle. She'd have no trouble killing a dhole, she said to Ying, and that would give them a breather. Firstly, it would show the dholes who was boss, and secondly, it would win them time because the other dholes would eat the carcass of their fellow. Things would be easier once it was daylight. Dholes were nocturnal, like foxes, and sunlight would give them a headache.

The heart was a strange thing. However great the terror, you could still it, by pretending. They were still surrounded by the enemy, their lives still hung by a thread, but they had stopped being so anxious. Lan Lan wanted a better look at their opponents. She turned the lamp down to its lowest and the darkness engulfed them. 'Shepherds carry firearms so much in the desert, the dholes must be scared stiff by them,' she said to Ying. Ying disagreed: 'It might be the first time they've seen a gun. If they were used to guns, they wouldn't run so far away.' Lan Lan had to agree.

Lan Lan raised the torch and swept its beam around them. She saw the dholes were all clustered to the east of them. At the top of the dune to the west, there were no black dots to be seen. They had chosen the usual place to camp, somewhere dry and out of the wind. The edge of a dune sheltered them to the west and in front of them lay a broad gully. 'That's not good,' said Lan Lan. 'If they climb up the west side, they just have to tumble down the slope to land right on top of us. I wouldn't even have time to pull the trigger.' We ought to move into the centre of the gully. They'll have to go further to reach us then, whatever direction they're coming from, and we'll be ready for them.'

Firing off the gun gave them a moment's grace. Lan Lan lit a big piece of firewood and made another fire in the centre of the gully. Then the girls sneaked over to it, with the pack loads, their bedding, the brushwood and the camels. But within an hour, the dune to the west of them was filled with black dots. Ying felt that if they hadn't moved, the dholes wouldn't necessarily have dared to move to the western dune because they would have been within range of the gun. Where they were now, they could be attacked from all sides.

And now that they had moved further from their shelter, they felt the desert wind more. Ying could feel the chill running down her spine. She opened the bag of spare clothes, got out two more jackets, put one round Lan Lan's shoulders and took one for herself. They still had their backs to the camels but the beasts were getting restless now. Obviously they could see the dholes on the western slope too. 'We shouldn't have moved,' said Ying. 'There's good and bad in both,' said Lan Lan. 'If we'd stayed where we were, they could have rushed down the slope and attacked us. Now we're out in the open, and so are they. All in full view. At least we'll go down fighting, that's the important thing, and the worst that can happen is that we fill the dholes' bellies. I've been thinking, it's not so bad to die young and leave this sinful world behind. Whatever happens, you're going to be dead meat, you can't escape that, however heroic you act. The Buddha gave up his life to feed a tiger and cut off his flesh to feed an eagle, so by the same token, I ought to be willing to lie down and give myself up to feed the dholes. But I don't want to. It would be different if they were good creatures like sheep are. But they're not! They're evil, blood-sucking, gut-rippers!'

Lan Lan's words woke Ying to their situation. The dholes had confronted them for so long, she had almost forgotten how ferocious they were. If they rushed them in a growling snarling pack, she thought, they'd be reduced to two skeletons in no time at all. Her terror returned. Lan Lan smiled: 'What are you afraid of? For sure,

you're going to die sometime anyway. Whether you're afraid of
death or not, you die just the same. Whether you live happy or sad,
you still live. Of course, it's better to get some enjoyment out of life
if you can. I've thought about it, and I reckon we live through our
feelings. What we see as good or bad luck is really just how we feel
about life. If we feel good, then we feel we're lucky. If we feel good
all our lives, then we're lucky all our lives too. We can't change the
world, but we can change the way we feel, don't you think?'

Ying began to see Lan Lan in a new light. Her companion
seemed to have changed a lot recently. Ying couldn't have had those
thoughts herself. Thoughts like these, whether joyful or depressing,
came from Lan Lan's own heart. People have value because of their
feelings, thought Ying. If people really cultivated tranquillity, that
made them boring.

Lan Lan swept the torch beam over the western dune and the
dense cluster of black dots moved. She gave the torch to Ying to
hold, lay on her belly on the sand and took aim. There was a spurt
of flame from the barrel of the gun but no yelps of pain. All they
could see was the black dots scattering. 'Huh!' exclaimed Lan Lan.
'I missed. Just one ball-bearing goes further but it's harder to hit
the target. The pellets are better.' 'Don't keep shooting like that,'
said Ying. 'If you don't fire, they might still fear you. If you keep
going "bang, bang" like that, they'll stop being afraid.' But Lan Lan

loaded the gun again. 'I just want to show them who's the boss,' she said. 'But for some reason, my aim is getting worse and worse.'

Ying was right. You could keep a wolf at bay by picking up a straw if it thought it was a cudgel. But if you beat it with the straw, it would pretty soon call your bluff. This time when she fired, the dholes were only a bit panicked and quickly gathered again, nearer to their camp. They were used to the torch now too, and no matter how Ying wildly waved it around, they hardly shifted. It wouldn't be long before she and Lan Lan would be filling their bellies, Ying thought, now they were used to the gun shots and the bonfire. Would her beloved ever have imagined that she would end up in the jaws of a dhole, she wondered. What would he have felt if he knew? Would he have cried? Probably yes, but for how long? That she was hard put to say. She had seen plenty of loving couples where one partner died and the other soon cheered up after a bit of weeping. Ying was disheartened at the thought. If life was so pointless, why not fill a dhole's belly? She remembered her mother shouting angrily at her when she was little, that she was 'wolf fodder'! At the time, she quite liked being called wolf fodder. It sounded nice. But maybe her mum's anger had really brought this on her, and she was going to end up, if not in the belly of a wolf, then in a dhole. There wasn't much to choose between them apart from size and shape. They were all savage beasts.

She might as well die, she thought. It would be better than living and pining for that useless lover of hers.

Suddenly Lan Lan shouted: 'Quick! Keep the fire alight!' Ying woke from her daydreams to find the tiny flame was down to just a red glow. She used the lighter on some twigs but they were damp, and all they would do was hiss. Lan Lan passed her a dry branch and it caught. 'Keep the dry and the wet wood separate,' she said. 'Look at the way they're lined up, they've got designs on us. You put brushwood all around us and if they do attack, then we can light it.' She shone the torch around. But Ying was discouraged. 'Look at all those eyes clustered together. You can see the outlines of the ones nearest to us.'

'You look after the fire,' said Lan Lan. 'Whatever you do, don't let it go out. I'm going to fire again a few times. That'll scare them off, for sure.'

Suddenly the dholes set up an unearthly howling, as if a million rats had fallen into boiling soup.

Lan Lan fired off the gun again, but that didn't stop the dholes howling.

3

Lan Lan was completely focused on loading the gun and firing it. She turned the tilley lamp to its brightest. The dholes howled and wailed. They hadn't attacked yet, but they didn't scatter every time they heard a gunshot either. They must have lost their fear of the bangs. Imagine an animal the size of civet, prepared to take on a wolf in a fight over food and not back down. The dhole was one fearsome, cunning animal. Lan Lan kept firing sporadically and the pellets fell among the dholes, but they were clearly not as intimidated as they had been. Ying felt fear again, and Lan Lan looked panicky too. 'Save on the ammo,' Ying said. 'Hey! We brought plenty with us,' Lan Lan objected. 'We only have to make it last till daylight, then everything will be OK!' But Ying thought, if they don't go away when it gets light, what do we do then?

Every time she loaded the gun, it took a few minutes and, in that interval, the dholes skipped a little nearer, seeing how close they could get. Now they seemed more afraid of the fire than of the gun. They would have pounced long ago, thought Ying, if we didn't have fire.

Lan Lan suddenly had a bright idea. She watched the dholes creeping closer and took careful aim. She waited patiently for the boldest to come nearer and nearer, then, when they were only about ten metres from the fire, she calmly pressed the trigger. Several of the dholes yelped in pain, and gave blood-curdling screeches. They sounded angry more than anguished, as if it were an insult to be hurt like this-by two women!

One dhole retreated, limping. The others gave a few more howls, then quietened down. The shot had hit them where it hurt. Lan Lan was pleased. She loaded again. 'I'm going for the pellets,' she said. They don't go as far but you can cover a bigger area.'

The camels started snorting. Several more dholes appeared to the west of them, prancing around, this way and that, as if to tease them, or to avoid the pellets. Their movements were by nature playful. It was only when they were ripping the guts out of a big beast like an ox that they turned ferocious. Normally they frolicked as playfully as kittens. They were not particularly strong, it was their ability to spring that was terrifying. Their spring, together with their sharp teeth, made them deadly.

Lan Lan re-loaded. She held her breath and took aim at the leaping dots. To be honest, she hardly needed to aim. When the pellets left the gun, the spurt of flame from the gun barrel expanded to the size of a cartwheel. It was a pretty scary sight in the darkness.

When the dholes had pranced and growled near enough, she pressed the trigger again. To her dismay, all she heard was a strike. In her haste, she had forgotten the primer. A dhole heard the noise and, perhaps understanding what it meant, it charged. Ying shook with terror but remembered to shine the torch at it. It came quite near, raised its hackles and bared its teeth at them, the way a mother dhole might do, defending its pups. Luckily, just then, the flames from the fire flared up and it beat a retreat. If it had been braver, it could have pounced and taken a chunk out of one of them in no more than a few seconds. Ying had seen how fast they could run, as they streaked across the sand. She wanted to pull out her Tibetan hunting knife, but she would have had to put the torch down and was afraid it would charge again. The dhole gave a low growl. Its teeth were very white. Its eyes had a sinister glint in them, and no longer shone green. It was obviously the boldest of the pack. Dholes had sharp muzzles, a bit like foxes. Ying actually admired foxes, they were so sprightly, and there was something ethereal about them. Dholes, however, were just sinister. She felt she had never seen true savagery before now. There was savagery in its bared fangs, its low growls and its raised hackles.

The dhole growled again and came closer. It was clearly not intimidated by the fire any more. Just as some humans were wiser than others, some dholes were wiser than others too, and this one must have discovered that fire was nothing more than a paper tiger. Lan Lan's dad had told them about meeting a wolf who was no longer afraid of fire. It had been stalking him and his group and in panic they lit a fire, but the wolf simply leapt back and forth over the fire as if it was teasing them. If old Meng hadn't shot it, they would have been a goner. Ling Guan and his brothers and sisters would never have been born. Well, that might have been better for her, thought Ying. It didn't matter how much she had loved that scoundrel, Ling Guan, she hadn't been able to make him love her the same way. At that thought, Ying stopped being afraid of the dhole. She shouted: 'Be off with you, scoundrel!'

There was a burst of gunfire.

The cluster of pellets whistled on their way, zooming towards their target like honeybees to blossom, like hungry houseflies homing on foul blood, like a randy stallion leaping out of its corral, like ejaculated sperm surging towards the welcoming womb, like tadpoles joyfully freed from the entrapping mud into fresh water. The pellets shattered the pitch darkness. They entered the body of the dhole through the pupils of its eye. The dhole may have had a small heart but they had huge, bottomless eyes. The pellets were quite well aware of this and leapt for joy.

Ying felt the pellets wriggled their tails and looked around at her. It reminded her of her sweetheart reciting the line to her: 'How to stop that lovely amorous gaze before she goes...'

The moment the pellets struck home, the dhole's eyes widened. The dhole knew these flying red tadpoles were up to no good. Damn right they weren't. It only had time to give a few turns and stretch its leg and its eyes stared heavenwards.

'Get the knife ready,' Lan Lan said. 'They don't seem to be

afraid of the fire now.' She wiped the sweat from her face. Ying felt a chill run down her spine. She flashed the torch around, and saw they were surrounded by black dots.

The gun wasn't keeping the dholes at bay.

Lan Lan had no time to draw breath now. She loaded and fired, loaded and fired. The smell of gunpowder filled the air. She was past caring whether her shots found their target or missed. Load, fire, load, fire, to the east, to the west. At least whichever direction she fired in, the dholes drew back a few paces, but only a few. As soon as the firing stopped, they pressed closer again. Ying got out the paraffin for the tilley lamp. She thought at least she could pour some over the ring of firewood, if by any chance the dholes charged. And if they broke through, then she would light all the wood and jump onto the pyre and that would be the end of it. The strange thing was that she felt less fearful now. No matter how scared you were, you couldn't keep it up forever. The fear of dying had given way to the fear of ending up as a dog's dinner. She was revolted at the thought of her body ending up as food for these animals, sickened at the idea of them dribbling over her clean body. She retched and retched but nothing came up. The two women hadn't eaten anything all night and she was starving. The smell of gunpowder that enveloped them was almost choking too. She peered through the smoke and saw that the gunfire was not helping much. Every now and then, some dholes yelped in pain but the others paid no attention to the injured. They did move back a little, at the very instant that Lan Lan took aim, but it wasn't a proper retreat, still less a rout. There was a good reason why such small creatures were a match for animals a great deal bigger than they were. In a fight over food with wolves, even if their comrades were torn to pieces, they kept up the attack. A couple of tasty young women and some great camels would be no trouble at all.

Apparently carnivores all consider human flesh the tastiest because humans have a lot of fat. Even though the earth's guardian spirits had prohibited it, once a beast had tasted human flesh, it would succumb to temptation and certainly commit more crimes. In human laws, no matter how heavily protected that animal was, once it had eaten a human, it would have to be put to death. If it had eaten one, it could eat a hundred.

Had these dholes eaten a human?

The gunfire was sporadic. It took time to load the gun. First Lan Lan poured the gunpowder down the funnel into the barrel, then she poked it down firmly, packed the pellets in and some more gunpowder. Burst of fire was always followed by an interval and the dholes would start growling and prancing up and down, until, at the next gunshot, they would retreat in panic, but each time, less far.

Ying piled on the brushwood. The leaping flames reflected off the dholes' bared fangs. The girls could see that they were coming closer. True, they weren't leaping over the bonfire, at least not yet, but that was bound to happen sooner or later. Ying remembered that when she was little, fires were lit at the winter solstice and the village youths would jump over them. It was called 'burning off diseases'. It was believed that jumping over the fire cured you of anything. Ying was too scared to do it, the flames made her feel dizzy, though she admired the young men and women who leapt like leopards. Then, once, her mother had put her arms round her and they jumped the fire together. Ying had shut her eyes and screamed. The second time, she was braver, and kept her eyes open. After her mother had jumped with her the third time, Ying plucked up the courage to leap on her own. These dholes must be the same, she thought. They feared the fire now, but they'd get used to it and once they had lost their fear, they would attack.

And what then? She shivered in fear.

4

The gunfire was no longer having any effect on the dholes. Ying felt sure that Lan Lan had been wrong to move their camp. They were surrounded on all sides now. The gunfire only made the growling dholes shift on the spot.

Ying could hear the camels spitting from time to time. These ferocious predators clearly terrified them, but the dholes ignored the camels' snorting. The camels shook their heads violently trying to snap the tethering rope, but could not break free of the willow wands twisted around their noses. The bits of scrub they were tied to shook violently but it was no good, their delicate noses were no match for the tethers. Even if they broke their noses pulling free, they couldn't necessarily escape the dholes' jaws. The dholes now had the girls and the camels completely surrounded. The first camel to flee would become the dholes' prey. Finally, the camels calmed down and stopped pulling at their ropes. They carried on snorting threateningly. But Ying knew that a spitting camel would have no effect on dholes that were unafraid of gunfire.

The women were in a bad way. First, they were running out of firewood. It had looked like a big pile, but the fire was greedy and they had kept it going all night. How long before dawn broke? It was hard to judge time. Sometimes whole months flashed, other times even a single day seemed to drag. Ying was no judge of time. She had brought a watch, but it was in her bag with her money. Thinking of the watch reminded her of her money. It would be better to carry it on her person—it was the money for the camel salt. She got Lan Lan to pass her the torch, found her bag and hung it round her neck. She gave the bag a squeeze, and felt the coins. Then she laughed at herself. How could she be thinking of money when she couldn't take charge of her own life? She was money-obsessed. All the same, she kept the bag slung round her neck. If the dholes ate her, they could eat the bag too, she thought. If she managed to get away, then she would need the money. She took her watch out and looked at it. It showed nearly four o'clock in the morning. 'If we can hang on another hour or so, it'll be daybreak,' she said to Lan Lan.

Ying felt sorry she hadn't gathered more brushwood before it got dark. There was scrub in their gully, but the dholes were in possession of that. The circle around them was getting smaller and smaller. Going to get firewood meant braving the dholes' teeth. She collected what she had together, but it would hardly have covered a gravestone. That was an unlucky thought. Maybe she really was going to die. The thought didn't frighten her as much as it had done before. The way she looked at it, death itself was not frightening. In her mind, she bracketed the word together with food and clothes. It was being ripped to shreds by the dholes that she didn't want. Dholes loved offal and the thought of them making a large hole in her belly, poking their sharp muzzles inside her and ripping out her heart, liver and lungs turned her stomach. If she had known it would be like this, she would have died on the night of the rainstorm. Well, so be it, if she was devoured by a dhole, at least she would not leave a mangled corpse behind, for her parents to see. She would simply vanish off the face of the earth. Fine. Then it occurred to her that the dholes would gnaw her face to shreds once they had eaten her innards, and she shivered again. My beloved, she thought, if I can't give my beautiful body to you, let the dholes have it. She felt a malicious pleasure at the thought, and then the tears came.

'You let the fire go out!' said Lan Lan accusingly.

Ying wiped her tears away, threw on a few dry twigs and puffed until the flames curled up. Four of the dholes were very close. Lan Lan loaded the gun again and fired, bringing down two. But the other two didn't run away, they just snarled at Lan Lan, retreating a few steps only when Ying threw more brushwood on the fire and the flames leapt. At least the fire still instilled fear in them, but it was a pity that they had so little to feed it with. If it went out, even gunfire would not be enough to deter the dholes. Ying looked longingly at the sky. This might be the last time she saw it, she thought. The firelight made the stars seem as dim as the longing in her heart. If she vanished in a puff of smoke, would he go looking for her? She wondered. She imagined him riding out on his camel, following the ravine, calling her name and weeping bitterly. Too late, she muttered to herself. Why didn't you love and cherish me when you could? Life had so much to offer, but you didn't want it. When you did, it was gone. It doesn't matter how hard you look, you can sift through every grain of sand, but you won't find me. Ying felt as if she was playing a game of hide and seek with him. She hated him for not being there when she needed him, but was quite carried away by the idea of him searching. As she fed the fire, tears ran down her face. She had always been like this, easily moved by her own fantasies.

The firewood was finished.

The circle of dholes had grown tighter as the fire burned lower, so they must have seen that. They could certainly spot human beings' vulnerability. They set up a chorus of blood-curdling howls. Lan Lan was firing as before, but was slower to load the gun. She was not as cool as she looked. Ying, however, had grown calmer. In her mind's eye, she saw Ling Guan gazing at her. I must keep my self-control, she thought, even though I can't change my fate… No amount of crying would drive the dholes off. So, better not to cry. She saw the flames burning lower. The fire gave them light, and light was life and hope. It warmed them in the darkness, but it was going out. She heard the dholes' joyful barking. They were no longer measuring their opponents in terms of food. She could see that from the way they did not gobble up their comrades' carcasses. This confrontation had gone beyond merely filling their bellies. The gunfire and the firelight had clearly awakened some different quality in them.

The fire went out. The darkness pressed in on them, a ring of green orbs appeared around them. The torch beam and the gunfire no longer struck fear into the hearts of the dholes, who sensed imminent victory. Lan Lan was loading and firing almost lethargically. The dholes did not charge them immediately, they just gave a few yelps, as if still wary, or as if playing a game of cat-and-mouse. A chorus of yelps from a pack of dholes would strike terror into your heart. Think of the howl of a mad dog, or of a hungry wolf, a woman's screeching, a slaughterman's curses, all mixed up together. It seemed not to come from the throat, but to squeeze through the gap between their teeth. There was a liquidity in the sound too, and a sneering. Ying felt as if she had been plunged into a nightmare. The dholes moved slowly forward. The green gleam in their eyes rippled like water.

Ying just hoped that they would kill her with one bite to the throat, and not rip her innards out first. She could not bear the thought of having her body defiled while she was still alive. She thought of the camel that had died in the gully. She did not want to die like that, she would rather hang herself or throw herself in the well. She did not want her flesh befouled by shit or swarms of bluebottle maggots breeding in her body. The best way to die, she reckoned, was to eat a lump of opium. Opium might be evil, but at least you died in a haze of pleasant fantasies. And after all, all human life was a fantasy anyway, surging by like floodwater, defying all attempts to get a grip on it. That thing humans prized so much, life, was nothing but a feeling. And opium, although it put an end to a life which you no longer wanted or could put to use, could give you a good feeling and so was much the best way. Ying regretted she had not brought with her some of the pain-killing opiate they had had at home for her Han Tou's headaches. Afraid he would try to kill himself, she had hidden it in the dusty rafters. The trouble was that even if she had brought it and swallowed it, it wouldn't stop the dholes tearing into her innards or the bluebottles using her flesh to nurture their maggots. Ying almost retched again. Silently, she beseeched the dholes: Just eat my bones clean, don't leave anything to rot. She thought of Tibetan "sky burials" and the lamas chanting prayers over the body, calling on the eagles to strip the body of the deceased. It was said to be an omen, if the birds left anything on the bones, that the dead person would not be reincarnated. She found that amusing. Fate always played strange tricks on her, kept making her change her mind. Like after Han Tou died, when her mother-in-law wanted her to marry his brother, Mengzi, She first refused, because it seemed like a profanity. But when her own mother tried to marry her to that slaughterman, marrying Mengzi suddenly became the thing she most desperately wanted but could not have. She had started by being afraid of being eaten by the dholes, then praying to the dholes to lick her bones clean. How ridiculous. Life was a puzzling thing.

The green orbs came nearer. She could hear the dholes panting and fully expected them to charge. She had seen how they sprang at their prey, a step back, a leap forward, their teeth fastened in her throat and it would all be over. No more thoughts, no more pain, no more struggling. She imagined herself falling into a black void. Would she still feel anything? She did not know. She hoped so. The thought of losing all feeling made her heart lurch. Then she told herself it was pointless worrying. Anyway, perhaps after life was finished, there was something more beautiful to look forward to. Of course it was impossible to tell. She hoped that he would be there, in that after-life. No matter how good the after-life, it would be meaningless without him.

Looking at the encircling eyes, Ying straightened up and challenged them: Come on then! What are you waiting for?

She felt a sudden gust of wind.

5

To her surprise, there was a whooshing noise and the flames leapt skyward. There was a sharp smell of paraffin in Ying's nostrils, and the sudden heat singed some strands of her hair. The dholes yelped and backed away. Ying yelped in fright too. She saw Lan Lan brandishing the paraffin tin. The effect was dramatic. No wonder it had driven off the dholes.

'Don't just stand there,' said Lan Lan. 'Tear up the bedding and soak it in paraffin.'

Of course, thought Ying. They did still have something left to burn.

The knife was sharp and with a few slashes, they had reduced the tent and quilt to strips. Not small enough. They had to slash them crossways. Ying wondered how they would manage without bedding, if they ever managed to make their escape. She sprinkled paraffin on the cotton covers and the camel hair stuffing. They were using up the paraffin meant for the tilley lamp, of course, and they would not be able to travel by night without the lamp, but it was more important simply to survive. She lit the paraffin-soaked fabric. She had meant to make the fire on top of the embers of the previous bonfire, but changed her mind and threw the flaming bundle at the encircling dholes. The ball of flame flew through the air and landed on top of one of the dholes, setting its pelt on fire. The terrified animal yelped piteously and tore round in circles. The animals nearest to it stampeded in panic. The flames on its back went out as soon as the paraffin had burnt out, however. It was still alive but howling in agony.

'Good!' shouted Lan Lan. She put down the bag of gunpowder and lit the camel hair. She threw bundles of it at the dholes on the other three sides. It was a good tactic: The dholes scattered. But when they had gone twenty metres, they refused to retreat any further. They stood still, their green eyes challenging them.

'We're idiots to hang around here,' said Lan Lan. 'We've got to think of a way out.'

'I agree,' said Ying. She was being careful with the paraffin, pouring on just enough to make it catch alight. She got two plastic bags and divided the remaining camel hair between them. They would use these as hand grenades, to break out of the encirclement. They saddled the camels and tied down the loads. Lan Lan loaded the guns and hung the gunpowder bag around her neck. They each mounted a camel, a lighter and a bag of fur in their hands. Ying weighed her hunting knife in her hand. She was going to go down fighting.

Lan Lan led the way, shining the torch in front of them. The dholes watched warily and silently, scrambling away as Lan Lan drew close. Lan Lan was going to fire at them, but there seemed to be no need. She smiled with satisfaction. 'Take it easy,' she said to Ying. 'No need to hurry. If we trot, they'll think we're afraid.' She was ready to light a clump of camel hair and throw it when the moment was right, but she was worried that there would be too much wind if the camels trotted and the hair would not catch alight. 'Yes, let's go slowly,' she said, 'we can never outrun the dholes in any case.'

The camels, however, were keen to make a quick get-away. They snorted and honked. Lan Lan hauled on her camel's nose rope, and finally persuaded it to stop prancing and slow down.

The dholes were quiet now, and Lan Lan still didn't want to provoke them. As she coaxed her camel past the dholes, Ying got her lumps of hair ready and lit the lighter. That way, she would be ready to light and throw it if the dholes made one move against them. The dholes seemed to guess, and took a few steps back.

The torch illuminated the rolling shapes of the dunes ahead. To Ying's relief, there was a ray of light in the east, a gleam of hope. She was exhausted. At the peak of her anxiety, she had not felt it, but now her whole body was completely drained of energy. Her eyes began to close. For an instant, she thought she must have fallen asleep. She longed to sleep, dholes or no.

Lan Lan shone the torch behind them. Its beam showed a line of black dots which clumped together in the gully. The embers of the fire still glowed. The camel bells tinkled in the chill desert wind, which flowed over them and penetrated their very being. Ying liked this wind. She had sweated a lot and she was thirsty. She put the bundles of fur back in the bag and opened the plastic water container that hung from the saddle. She drank a few gulps and passed it to Lan Lan. Lan Lan hung the gun around her neck and drank too. She was normally very sparing with the water, but just now she felt she deserved a reward.

The cluster of black dots grew smaller. Ying heaved a sigh of relief. She was surprised that such savage animals had been so afraid of their gunpowder and fire balls. Perhaps it was just beyond their ken.

It was getting lighter in the east. The wind was raw, a Qilian Mountain wind, the villagers called it, whirling down from above. It came almost every morning and during the threshing season, the old villagers relied on it for their threshing. Ying felt her fatigue blow away. The camels snorted vigorously, and their strides lengthened. Lan Lan no longer hung onto the nose rope so hard. The more distance they put between themselves and those loathsome creatures they had left behind them, the better. Fine, she thought, and loosed the rope, kicking her mount into a gallop.

A hump looked like a steady place to sit, but a camel wasn't as smooth a ride as a horse. When a horse galloped, you only rose and fell gently, but on a camel, you got bounced up and down. Ying tied the plastic bag with the camel hair in to the packsaddle and gripped the hump with both hands. She hoped the camel wasn't going to bolt. If it did, she wouldn't be able to control it.

Lan Lan could see Ying was anxious and slowed her beast. The gun was bouncing around on her chest. She held it steady with one hand, while the other hand pulled on the rope. Her camel obediently came to a halt. Ying's camel caught up, and slowed down too.

But they could still hear the dholes. Ying hurriedly pulled out the paraffin-soaked camel hair and tried to light it. But the wind kept blowing out the lighter flame. Finally she succeeded in lighting the bundle of hair and throwing it behind them but the dholes simply dodged it. They were unconcerned, but the camel pranced in fright. Lan Lan raised the gun and pointed it behind, but when she pressed the trigger, there was only a click. The jolting had bounced the gunpowder out of the barrel.

Ying kept pressing the lighter, and each time the flame was extinguished by the wind. In any case, no flaming ball of hair was going to stop the dholes. The desert was big and all they had to do was dodge it. Ying put the lighter and the camel hair away. She gripped the hump with one hand and her knife with the other. There was nothing for it, she thought, but to go for broke. Lan Lan was having no luck loading the gun either. The gunpowder was simply shaken out of the barrel, and she gave up. She did not need to urge the camel to go faster, it was gathering speed anyway. Saving themselves depended on how fast their camels went. They both knew that dholes were amongst the desert's fastest animals. It would be hard to out-run them.

Ying had ridden camels, but they were properly broken-in

beasts, that went at a walking pace. She had never galloped along like this. Panic-stricken, she lay back against the packsaddle. The bumping hurt her tail-bone even though she was cushioned by the remaining bedding. Lan Lan was a toughie, she thought. She had shredded her sleeping mat to burn and all she had underneath her were the felt saddle bags. Since lighting the balls of camel hair could not stop the dholes, she unfastened the plastic bag, kicked her camel forward until it caught up with Lan Lan's and handed it over. 'Sit on this,' she said.

Almost without them noticing, the sky had turned completely light. Ying could see that the dholes were pursuing them, but warily, as if they suspected them of having a secret weapon in their hands. That was good. Also, the girls could not hear them so clearly, what with the sounds of the wind and the clattering of their cooking utensils. 'Don't be afraid!' shouted Lan Lan. 'Once the sun is up, the dholes will get lost. Just concentrate on staying on your camel.' She was being kind-hearted, but it just made Ying more worried that she might fall off. In that case, the dholes would have their teeth into her straightaway. She was most afraid that the camel might stumble and break a leg in one of the desert rat burrows that were dotted all over the sands. There were plenty of rat burrows on the shaded slopes, but Lan Lan kept urging her camel in that direction. Not that it made any difference to the dholes, but on the sunny, south-facing slopes, there was a lot of loose sand and with one careless step, a camel could take a tumble.

It looked like the dholes were not going to give up on the prospect of a free meal. They could see that the girls had no new tricks up their sleeve, and were content to lope along behind them. They came closer and closer, and the camels were beginning to panic. If they carried on running like this, they might trip and fall. This was terrible. She felt mentally drained by her fear. She just had to leave it to the camel. She could hear the aggressive yapping of the dholes. If they put on a spurt and then outflank us, she thought, it's all over.

Ying saw the plastic bag with the camel hair go flying, as Lan Lan threw it away. It provided a momentary distraction as the dholes swarmed over it and pulled it to pieces. Ying suddenly had a thought: Lan Lan's gambit was a useful one, even though it had only halted the dholes briefly. She hung onto the hump with one hand and, with the other, fumbled for the bag of cooking stuff. In spite of all her efforts, she couldn't manage to undo it. At that moment, a dhole came level with them, bouncing and snarling menacingly. She slashed at the bag and heard the pan, bowls and chopsticks clattering to the ground with a terrific noise. That did give the dholes a fright. They all skidded to a halt.

'Right,' said Lan Lan. 'Throw away what we don't need, and

save ourselves.'

Ying was disappearing into the distance. 'Throw your spare clothes out!' Lan Lan shouted after her. 'Just keep the water and the buns. When they catch up, throw something at them. Our lives are the most important thing.' Ying fumbled around, and finally pulled out some spare clothes. There was fierce yelping coming from behind her.

The sun poked half a head above the horizon. The dholes were not the slightest bit worried about the burning white disc which rose above the earth. The chase turned into a farce. The dholes were fascinated by the clothing the girls discarded, and as soon as a garment floated down, they swarmed around it and tore it to shreds. The bits of coloured fabric looked like butterflies. Garment after garment landed in front of the dholes and they were interested in everything. As if they were aware that their opponents had no more tricks up their sleeve, they seemed content to play games for the time being, prancing and snarling around each item. Ying knew that the game with her clothes put off the moment when they would die, but she was still sorry to see them go. Finally, all she had left was a blue jacket, given to her by Ling Guan, the proof of his love. She refused to throw that down to them. If she had to die, she would die with it. And she put the jacket on.

Lan Lan threw down all sorts of stuff too, all useful things, but they would have no more opportunity to make use of it. The sun rose till its rays reached halfway up the poplar trees. There had been no rosy dawn. That meant it was going to be a scorcher today. The dholes seemed not to care, though. 'I'm lost,' said Lan Lan, 'but if we just follow the track east, we might meet some herders, and we can ask the way.' The problem was that they could not shake off the dholes. Their pursuers were tired of ripping up the clothes, and everything else they threw down seemed just to make them yelp more viciously. It sounded as if they knew all there was to know about the girls and their camels, and knew they would not be providing any new amusements.

They were closing in for the kill.

6

The dholes streaked along like the wind, their yelps reverberating through the gully.

Ying couldn't be bothered to go on throwing anything down, since the dholes had lost interest. The end was getting closer, and she felt filled with leaden-grey thoughts, the kind she always got when she was in despair. Everything in the world looked grey, and turned dream-like: The dholes' yelps, the jolting hillocks of the dunes, even Lan Lan, who had been her sole source of comfort in their flight. Who would have thought they would end up like this? A wave of desolation surged over her, rather like the sadness of the Gansu epic ballads, Xian Xiao. She remembered that Ling Guan liked these epics, with their sonorous rhythms. She found them crude. How ridiculous to be thinking about Xian Xiao when they were in such a predicament. The notes of the songs were like wisps of smoke curling up from the sands. Everything seemed more dream-like than ever. She looked around vaguely, to see the dholes bouncing along behind her like fleas in a hot pan. Blood-thirsty creatures. Strangely, all she felt was utter exhaustion, an exhaustion that turned everything into a dreamscape and she herself into a shadow.

The camels jolted them up hillocks and down slopes. If they trip and fall, so be it, she thought. Sooner or later, it was going to happen. But her head thought one thing, and her body another: All by itself, it leaned forward and clung like a limpet to the camel's hump. Ling Guan always used to say the body was the fortress of the spirits, but just now she lacked the energy to pray to the spirits inside her. Have it your own way, she addressed them. If you want to be food for the wolves, that's fine.

It was quieter behind, either because the noises had really ceased, or because she was imagining it, but she could no longer hear them in any case. She could not even hear the camels panting or the wind in her ears. Everything seemed crystallized. She was still aware of the jolting motion, in a shadowy sort of way. The melodies of the Xian Xiao kept going round and round in her head, and in the resonant chords of the three-stringed *san xian zi*, she sensed a kind of spiritual struggle. This was real music, she thought, a spiritual music which had grown up over a thousand years.

She had no more strength left. She wished she could just fall asleep perched on the camel. She didn't care anymore that the dholes would rip out her guts or gnaw her flesh. But although her body was exhausted, her mind was crystal-clear. Her dreaminess was really clarity. Ling Guan used to say that all human life was a dream. It seemed improbable to her, as she held his warm, living body in her arms. Now she believed him. Everything really was a dream, her distant parents, the dholes pressing closer, the jolting camel hump, even her body, bouncing up and down in the air. Most dream-like of all were the notes of the *san xian zi*.

'Was this what people felt when they turned their back on this world and became a monk or a nun?' she wondered. 'Did they feel that everything had crumbled to dust, and become a dream? But they did not reject the world completely,' she knew that. Something held them in it by a gossamer thread.

Lan Lan slowed down, pulling on the nose rope to make sure Ying did not fall behind. But her camel had other ideas. Even if it could not out-run the dholes, it was faster than its companion. Ying was grateful when Lan Lan hauled it back to keep pace with her. She felt profoundly lucky that she had ended up with a sister-in-law who was willing to share life and death with her.

Lan Lan gave a shrill cry in an attempt to scare the dhole, or perhaps to draw them off Ying and towards her. Ying smiled wryly. The creatures were not even afraid of a gun, so no amount of shrieking would scare them. She shouted to Lan Lan: 'Forget about me, make a break for it! At least then one of us will be safe.' 'Don't be an idiot!' Lan Lan said. 'And stop fretting. When the sun's high in the sky, they'll get a headache and go to ground.' Ying knew this was intended to comfort her. True, foxes got a headache in the sunshine, but not dholes.

Ying looked back to see the dholes bouncing along, closer and closer. The closest were only twenty feet away. She could even see their greedy eyes and bared fangs, and the dust they kicked up behind them. Terror, numbed by her daydreams, swamped her again. She could not bear the thought of being bitten by those filthy teeth. It was worse than death itself. She felt a surge of loathing for the dholes, where just a few moments ago she was resigned to her fate. She gripped the knife hard. I'll go down fighting, she vowed. She patted the camel. Mind how you go, she told it, don't stumble. I'll make the dholes taste my knife. The beast gave an answering snort, as if to reassure her.

Ying forced herself back to reality. Daydream was dangerous. The dholes of course didn't care, one way or the other, they wanted to taste real flesh. And death was very real. Her mother and father had given her such a fine body, how could she simply hand it over to the dholes? The thought of her mother made tears of remorse run down her face. She shouldn't have said those things to her. If she survived, she would cook her chilli tripe every day. She would even sell her blood to get the money for the chilli tripe.

She heard a shout from Lan Lan: 'Stab it!' She turned and saw a dark shape springing at her. Without pausing to think, she brought the hunting knife down hard, felt it make contact, and heard a howl of pain. The dhole rolled down into the gully. 'Well done!' shouted Lan Lan. 'One less dhole!' Ying looked at the knife in surprise. There was blood on it. She wondered how she had managed to stab and kill it so easily. Of course, she thought, it was only the size of a civet. She felt filled with courage. Another dhole behind that one was jumping at the camel's belly and she stabbed at it. But although she tried several stabs, she missed each time.

Lan Lan steadied herself and managed to push the funnel into the barrel. That was better, even if some of the powder was shaken out, some, at least stayed down. As she packed and poked the barrel, she yelled furiously at the dholes, the way she used to yell at vicious dogs in the village.

More dholes caught up with Ying. She took her courage in her hands and whirled and stabbed with the knife, the way they did it in films. Although she didn't hit home, her stabs kept them at bay. They yelped and leapt into the air, clearly trying to intimidate her. Ying was scared, but carried on hacking as hard as ever. Unfortunately the camel panicked, and started to veer this way and that. Ying was worried it might bolt, and hauled on the halter rope. With great difficulty, she managed to make it keep pace with Lan Lan's camel.

A dhole saw its chance and leapt at Ying, evidently aiming for her knife hand. It miscalculated and landed on the camel's tail. Ying slashed savagely at it. The blow went home, but unfortunately she managed to slash the camel's rump as well. The blood spurted out and the camel was even more panicked.

The smell of blood maddened the dholes and they surged forward as a pack. It was obvious that they were trying to bring down her camel. The camel sensed it and swerved away. 'Hang onto its neck!' shouted Lan Lan. But it was too late. Ying felt herself being propelled, somersaulting, through the air. She shut her eyes and let herself roll. Waves of sand hit her in the face. It's over, she thought. I've fallen into the dhole's jaws. 'Mum!' she screamed. It was an instinctive cry, and did not seem to matter that she'd rowed so bitterly with her mother recently.

7

'Quick! Quick!' Lan Lan shouted.

Ying stopped rolling over the sand, and opened her eyes to see two sturdy camel legs and Lan Lan's outstretched hand. She grasped the hand and got to her feet. 'Climb up! Quick!' shouted Lan Lan. Ying hung on, and stepped on the foot Lan Lan held out for her. With some difficulty, she scrambled up behind Lan Lan. Her own camel had fallen and the dholes were swarming all over it. She heard its shrieks of pain but Lan Lan said: 'We can't do anything for it. Its leg is broken. It trod in a rat burrow.'

One dhole left the fallen camel and approached them, but Lan Lan knocked it to the sand with her gun. She was in no hurry now. The dholes had a whole camel to eat. It would provide them with a meal for quite some time.

Ying was horror-struck. Lan Lan's dad had loved that camel. He'd paid 4,000 yuan for it and had no intention of parting with it. It would have been better to feed herself to the dholes. She watched, stunned, as the still-screaming camel was ripped apart by the dholes, and tears poured down her face. 'I should have died instead!' she cried. Lan Lan tried to comfort her: 'Don't say stuff like that! People are what count. If the two of us live, don't you think we can buy him another camel?'

Ying suddenly felt the desert wind penetrating right through her clothes. She felt chilled to the bone. The camel was silent now, and lay still, its legs sticking out, on the desert sand. It was almost invisible under the dholes—all you could see were its hooves. The dholes were completely absorbed and paid no more attention to Ying and Lan Lan. Ying thought of the camel which just a few minutes before had been carrying her along, now reduced to a lump of flesh, and felt herself in a dream world again.

Lan Lan finished loading the gun. She sighed and said, 'Come on, let's go.'

She loosed the nose rope. The camel turned, without needing any encouragement, and jolted and bumped away. It must have been shocked by what had happened to its mate. Its coat was covered in sweat but, spurred on by the memory of the dholes' sharp teeth, it put on a burst of speed.

Ying wiped her tears away. There was no point in crying, she thought.

'It's a pity about the water,' sighed Lan Lan. 'The rest doesn't matter. Well, we'll just have to make do with the water we've got.'

It was as if her words opened the floodgates of hunger and thirst. They drank a little water, and ate some bread. 'It was a good thing Dad knows about desert travel,' said Lan Lan. Her father had made them split their supplies into two and carry half each. 'As if we weren't being punished enough,' said Ying bitterly. 'Oh don't worry,' said Lan Lan. 'We've got gunpowder. If we come across a rabbit or something, I might get a pot shot at it. I could shoot two... haven't you ever eaten roast rabbit? It's a lot better than yams. Every cloud has a silver lining,' and Lan Lan pulled a funny face.

Ying wasn't at all sure about the silver lining. The dholes might come after them again, once they had eaten their fill of the camel.

Now that the tension had relaxed, they were overwhelmed with sleep and rode along flopping from one side to the other. Lan Lan tried to stay awake, afraid that the camel would go off course. Although they were lost, in an area they had never been before, it didn't matter too much, Lan Lan felt, providing they kept going east. To the east lay Mongolia, and human habitation. They needed to meet other people. One person's food between two would only keep them going a few days. They couldn't afford to meet any more obstacles and spend time going out of their way, or they would end up as dried-up corpses.

The camel was puffing and panting harder now. It had gone a long way and was now carrying two people. Besides, it was due for another feed. Without the energy it could draw from its hump, it would have been quite spent. Lan Lan knew they needed to find somewhere where the beast could eat and they could drink more water. Ying was asleep, slumped against her. Lan Lan was worried that they might both fall off if they didn't get some rest soon.

As they crossed a ridge, they came across some needlegrass which, although withered, would do for the camel to eat. A camel could eat almost anything that grew in the desert. Lan Lan shook Ying awake and they both got down. Without bothering to take the pack saddle off, Lan Lan tethered the camel and she and Ying dropped to the sand. They were asleep before they had a chance even to stretch out.

Lan Lan was woken by the sun's heat. She did not know how much time had passed, but she was covered in sweat and her eyes and throat burned. The sun was nearly at its zenith and not a breath of wind stirred in the gully.

The camel had vanished.

Lan Lan was alarmed. She prodded Ying to wake her. 'The camel's run off,' she said. She was a tough woman, but now there was a sob in her voice. Ying was dreaming that she was partying with the dholes but, at the sound of Lan Lan's voice, she woke up, her mouth dry with fear. This was the end, then, she thought. The camel's taken all our food and water. We won't last long now, will we?

They set off in search of it. They followed its footsteps, still clear in the sand because it was a windless day. The footprints, sometimes deep, sometimes shallow, stretched away to the horizon.

If the camel really wanted to get away from them, they would never catch it, Lan Lan grumbled to herself. Foxes weren't the only creatures that knew how to cover their tracks. Camels could keep going on and on, if they wanted. It was always said that camels were so accustomed to humans that they rarely ran away. Camels also knew that in the fine-sand desert, it was a betrayal to run away from their masters, especially if you were carrying their food and water. But this beast had been borrowed from another villager. It did not belong to Lan Lan's family. A family camel would be fond of her. She could not forgive it for running away. She felt overwhelmed with pity for the other camel, her own. It had been the best in the village. When two wolves had attacked it by biting its hump, it killed them and the villagers crowned it the Camel King. Whoever would have thought it would end up as a meal for the dholes?

They wore themselves out looking for the camel. Had it gone looking for food and water? Or was it running away? Lan Lan wondered. If it was running away, there was absolutely no point in them looking for it. They flopped onto the sand, and caught their breath. 'We shouldn't give up until we're really done in,' said Ying. So they got to their feet and carried on tracking the prints, up the hills and down the gullies. But all they found was a bun that had rolled out of its pack. Of the camel, there was no trace.

Lan Lan wiped the sweat from her face and said: 'Too bad it

wasn't this one that got fed to the dholes. The one that deserved to live, died and the one that deserved to die, lived. It's too bad.' 'We have to keep going,' said Ying. 'The bag of buns must have had a hole in it. If we don't find the camel, at least we'll find more buns.' 'I wouldn't put it past that damned beast to eat the buns it dropped,' grumbled Lan Lan. And, sure enough, they did come across a pile of half-eaten buns.

'I've had enough. Let's stop,' said Lan Lan.

8

This was a terrible blow. Things were very bleak. With the camel gone, they had no food or water. The food didn't matter. At a pinch, they could always eat the desert rice that grew on the fine-sand, and they wouldn't starve. But without water, they could not survive. The merciless rays of the sun licked at your skin until your blood coagulated and dried up completely. Then all that survived was your spirit. Your body could not obey you. Ying remembered what dried green beans looked like. They always had bugs that had bored their way inside. When she spread the beans out in the courtyard to dry in the sun, the bugs played dead, and you might take them for seeds. But Ying never bothered whether they were bugs or seeds, because the sun baked them anyway. Now she and

Lan Lan were going to turn into dried-up bugs. Was this retribution, she wondered? She baked the bugs and she was going to be baked. She had sweated so much, she was seriously dehydrated, and her blood must be viscous. It was not surprising that the camel had run off in fright. The humans were scared, and the future held unknown terrors. No wonder it was scared too.

Lan Lan and Ying sat on the sand and the sun burned down on them. Neither of them had anything to say. The camel had taken with it everything that could have kept them alive. They couldn't go far now. With every step, they lost water through sweat and through the sun. Disasters never came singly.

When they still had the camel, even though they were thirsty, they could get by, just sipping a little water now and then. But now they craved water. Every cell of their bodies was parched. Ying could even hear her cells breaking down from thirst. It was a crackling sound, like when you walked barefoot through wheat stalks. The dholes seemed to be scrabbling in her throat with their claws, and maggots squirmed there as if stuck fast in glue. The thought made her feel sick. She tried not to think about it, but her body disgusted her. When they were battling with the dholes, at least they could see the enemy, and sometimes land a blow on them. Now they didn't know where the enemy was. The blistering sun with its glaring white rays was one, but there was no point pitting your strength again the sun. Then again, fate itself was an enemy. It had an irresistible energy that you could not escape from, no matter how hard you tried to wriggle out of its clutches. You couldn't get to grips with fate, but the enemy that you could see and touch was your own body. When you thought about it, all the struggles were for your body, to feed and clothe it. Forget about your soul, all the pain and suffering you endured was for the sake of your body. If it were not for those rapturous kisses and physical intercourse, she wouldn't miss her body at all. And now this body of hers was tormenting her.

Ying lay on the sand and stared helplessly at the sky. The sun blazed down onto her face. She had always taken care of her skin, and shaded it from the sun's rays. If you got too sun-burnt, the melatonin gave you dark blotches. But if they were going to die of thirst, it didn't matter what her face looked like, she was still going to turn into a mummy or be ripped to shreds and devoured by wild beasts. Just bake me, sun, she said to herself. Spare me any more suffering. If she was mummified and buried in the sand, maybe in a thousand years, someone would dig her up, maybe even display her in a museum. Ling Guan had once seen a mummified woman in the Liangzhou Museum and told her she was very ugly. No one could know whether she had ever loved, or indeed what kind of life she had led, and the mummy wasn't talking. Her entire life was a mystery, and unravelling it had defeated all the scholars' efforts. If she were dug up a thousand years later, she would be a riddle too, Ying thought. No one would be able to tell that she had loved, that she had enjoyed physical ecstasy with a young man called Ling Guan. No amount of scholarship would be able to shed light on that secret. She felt quite gleeful about that. She smiled slyly to herself. Just you try, just you run yourselves into the ground trying. None of you will ever be able to see into my heart. None of you will ever know how I loved him. She could almost see the scholars looking mortified at their failure, and smiled.

Then another thought occurred to her: If no one wrote about her love, wouldn't that be the same as if her love had never existed? Just like flowers that bloomed in remote mountains might just as well never have bloomed if no humans ever saw them? The thought made her anxious. Even if she had concealed that love from everyone around her, at some point far in the future, someone ought to write about passions like hers. Otherwise, such love would be like flowers blooming where no one ever went. There had to be a way to tell those who came after about her love.

She racked her brains, but could not think of a way to do it. If there was a stone around, she could have scratched characters on it with her hunting knife. She even knew what characters she would scratch. She searched and searched, but could not find a stone.

There was only sand, and sand was untrustworthy. You could write your absolute undying loyalty on it, and with a gust of wind, the surface of the sand would be wiped clean. Oh, if only she could find a stone! But stones were like your hopes for a good life-they only turned up when you weren't looking for them. Finally, she thought of a way. Last year, some ancient objects from the Western Xia Dynasty had been excavated from the Vajravarahi Caves in Gansu. Mostly they were garments of fine silk, with embroidery so fine that they had the experts clicking their tongues in admiration. It was only the aridity of the desert sands that had saved them. In a more humid area, they would have perished long ago. Even if they weren't a thousand years old, the garments could easily date back a few hundred years. Not that it mattered whether the clothes were a hundred or a thousand years old, to a dead person, it was all the same.

She decided to write something with her blood on her clothing. She put her finger in her mouth and gave it a hard bite. She had always been afraid of pain, and it caught her up in it like a whirlwind. She thought, if such a little bite causes me so much pain, what agonies must the camel eaten alive by the dholes have felt? She shivered, feeling guilty. If only she had urged it forward, the way Lan Lan had done with hers, it might not have caught foot in a rat hole and broken its leg. Then she pulled herself together. She had something to do, and she had to get on with it! She pulled out her knife and ran her finger over the blade.

The blood oozed slowly from the wound, and Ying took off her blue jacket and wrote on it with the blood. But she only managed one stroke of the first character before the blood dried up. It really was very thick. She remembered how she used to be afraid of bleeding. When she bled, it wouldn't stop. The doctor told her she didn't have enough blood platelets and advised her to eat peanut skins. Now the thing she most wanted was to bleed more so that she had enough blood to finish, but maddeningly, the blood had congealed. She sucked and sucked, and finally got a few more drops out. Sucking and writing, sucking and writing, she finally succeeded in writing what she wanted to say. It was only a few characters, clumsily written, but at least they were legible:

'Ying loves Ling Guan.'

It did not matter, she thought, whether it took a hundred or a thousand years for someone to find this. They would immediately know that her name was Ying and that she had loved a man called Ling Guan. That would mark her mummified corpse out from the museum specimens. Who knows, perhaps some well-intentioned writer might create moving stories on the basis of these words. The hero of the stories would be Ling Guan, the heroine, Ying. In her mind's eye, she could see the TV drama a hundred years hence, and the eyes of the audience brimming with tears. Strangely, the thought made her own eyes brim with tears.

The tears fell silently. She wiped them away, satisfied with what she had done.

Ying was easily moved to tears. Even novels made her cry. Odd that she didn't feel so thirsty any more. The effect of art, perhaps?

Suddenly a terrible thought struck her. Would the clothes, with their message, survive if she was eaten by a wild beast?

9

She was plunged into despair. Just because you wanted something to last forever, it didn't mean it would. She had often seen the tattered remnants of clothing, torn to shreds by wild animals, on the river bank near the village, as well as fragments of bones they had gnawed. That was how she would end up, she was sure, if she died here. Apart from the dholes, there were wolves, desert rats and other animals with sharp teeth. What a lot of sharp teeth there were in the world. Well, that was just the way it was. Humans were brought into this world to suffer, so there had to be lots of creatures that caused them suffering.

She was anguished at the thought that such a beautiful love story might be buried and lost in the sands. It was worse than dying.

Suddenly the words 'lost in the sands' brought a fleeting thought into her head. She grasped at it. It was this: If she were to bury herself in the sands, no wild animal would find her.

It gave her a frisson of excitement.

That was a good idea. After all, all those excavated cultural objects had been preserved in the desert sands and the loess earth for a thousand years. She looked around her and her eyes settled on a steep sandy slope. Since she had to die, it would be much better to bury herself alive than to die of thirst. The pain would not last long. But dying of thirst would be agonizing.

She was in no hurry. She would wait until all hope was exhausted and she was close to death. Then it occurred to her that when she was close to death, she would not have the strength to bury herself. I have the strength now, she thought, I'll dig the hole now. Then all she had to do, when the moment came, was step into it and hope that the sand would collapse over her and bury her.

She dragged herself to her feet and went to the slope. It was pretty high. She chose the steepest bit and began to dig the sand with her hands. Lan Lan had her eyes shut, day-dreaming about something or other. She opened them and glanced at Ying, but did not ask what she was doing. Perhaps she thought Ying was digging a hole to sleep in.

Ying carried on digging. She worked carefully. It was not heavy work, but the difficulty was that, as well as making the hole, she had to make its edges overhang, not too much, but enough so that when she stepped in, the sand would collapse on top of her. This required some care but Ying succeeded. However a feeling of disappointment crept over her as she dug. She discovered that under the surface, the sand was damp. That meant that the jacket on which she had written the characters would rot.

Suddenly she felt completely discouraged.

Everything's against me, she thought. I can't even find a dry spot for my corpse.

At some point, Lan Lan appeared behind her, and she heard a shout:

'Reed rhizomes!'

10

'You know what reed rhizomes are?' Lan Lan was excited. 'The roots of reeds, obviously. But they're also the first thing that the Taoist sages found when they went in search of the Earth's Dragon Veins. Dragons Veins Beards, they call these reeds.' Ying could not help being infected by Lan Lan's mood. Lan Lan didn't get excited easily, there must be a good reason for it. Then she remembered Old Meng the hunter saying that Dragon Veins were actually underground watercourses. That meant that they could dig under the reed rhizomes and find water. Digging in the desert and finding water...what ecstasy!

Ying perked up, even though Lan Lan hadn't bothered explaining what Dragon Veins were. She assumed that everyone from Liangzhou knew they meant water. Of course they were more than that, they were places where the *yin-yang* was especially good and very fine people were produced, and so on, but Lan Lan wasn't bothered about that either. In her eyes, reed rhizomes were food, water, life itself. She bent down and tugged at the reeds with both hands, kicked away the sand and pulled out two rhizomes. She gave the longest one to Ying. 'Look,' she said, 'There's a lot of water in them. Don't spit out any of it, chew it up and swallow it.' Ying bit into it and cool liquid flooded her mouth. It was a wonderful feeling. She had never tried reed rhizomes before and, at first glance, had taken them for bits of driftwood. They certainly didn't look as if they had this much sap in them. She thought she had never tasted anything as good.

Lan Lan munched some herself and jumped into the ditch Ying had dug. She traced the stems in the sand, digging down until she got to the roots, and threw them out, in a pile. 'Don't eat them all at once, keep some for later,' said Lan Lan. The reed rhizomes were plump and pale, and temptingly full of sap. Ying couldn't resist taking a few more mouthfuls. She felt as if her throat had grown arms and they were reaching for more. She got a plastic bag out of her pocket, wrapped the buds in toilet paper and put them in the bag, where the desert wind could not dry them up. Another lifeline, she thought, it's true there's always a way out. Just when you think you've reached the end of the road, you find things are looking up.

The pile was getting bigger. Reed rhizomes were like Chinese liquorice roots, they put down runners. Once you found one runner, you could follow the root system and pull lots more out. In folklore, the reed rhizomes that grew on the imperial tombs had root systems that were hundreds of miles long. Once the 'dragon energy' seeped into a family's grave, that family would produce an emperor sooner or later. The crescent dunes were places where a dragon vein had been chopped off by the emperor. The people who live there regarded the reed rhizomes as auspicious: You congratulated the families on whose tombs they grew.

Ying could hear Lan Lan panting, down in the ditch. She kept throwing more rhizomes up, until the plastic bag filled up. 'You take a rest,' said Ying. 'Let me have a go.' Lan Lan wiped her sweaty face and smiled. 'I'm fine,' she said. 'I'm not tired. However did you think of doing this?' Ying could think of no way of explaining why she had dreamed up the idea, so she smiled and said nothing. But Lan Lan was not paying attention, in any case. She was clearly thrilled at her discovery. If only they had a shovel, thought Ying. That would have been even better. Then she thought she was being greedy. Wasn't it enough to have the reed rhizomes, without wanting a shovel too? If you had a shovel, you'd want a tent next, and then a fancy car. And the more you had, the more you worried. Better stick to reed rhizomes. Just now, they were manna from heaven.

The plastic bag was full. Ying wanted to find something else to put the roots in, and Lan Lan threw down her headscarf. They wore them over their heads to keep the burning sun off. She remembered that they had a square of cotton as well, with the rolls wrapped in it. Or rather, they didn't have it any more because it was in the saddlebag of the runaway camel. Forget it.

Ying was about to take Lan Lan's place when she suddenly saw sand trickling from the sides of the hollow. 'Get out!' she shouted at Lan Lan. 'The walls are giving way!' Lan Lan got up and was about to jump out when the walls gave way on top of her. She fell backwards and was covered in sand. It kept pouring in.

Ying was terrified. She grabbed Lan Lan's arm and hauled on it. But the more she pulled, the faster the sand poured over Lan Lan's shoulders. Lan Lan's mouth was open and she was gasping for breath. Ying didn't dare pull harder, and Lan Lan didn't dare move. After a little while, the sand slowed to a trickle and stopped.

Ying did not know what to do. Lan Lan was in great danger. If more sand fell in, it would be soon over her head. The sand would fill her ears, nose, mouth, and anywhere else it could get to, and that would be the end of her. Even if she could dig her out in time, Lan Lan would suffer serious effects from inhaling sand.

'Don't move!' she ordered. She was worried that if Lan Lan struggled, it would set off another sand-slide. And the Sand Dragon had no shortage of sand at its disposal. If you provoked the Sand Dragon, it could smother you in the stuff. People who lived in this desert all believed in the Sand Dragon. Its realm was the sand, just as the Black Dragon's realm was water. It claimed those buried in sand-slips, and the Black Dragon claimed the drowned. A long time ago, there was a temple to the Sand Dragon in their village, where the villagers all went to pay their respects on the fifteenth day after the new year. The Sand Dragon got angry with those who did not. But times changed. In the old days, virgin boys and girls were sacrificed to the Sand Dragon, then it was sheep and oxen. And finally the Red Guards pulled the Sand Dragon Temple down. Ever since then, the old people said, the sands had crept closer and closer to the village, burying a lot of land on its way. Ying had never believed in spirits but just now, she would have believed in anything, even a dog, if it could have saved Lan Lan. She implored the Sand Dragon not to carry her off. Lan Lan herself was saying a silent prayer to Vajravarahi. She made a huge effort to keep calm, even though the pressure of the sand was making it difficult for her to breathe. She knew that no amount of panicking would save her now.

The sand could start to slip again at any time, she thought. She needed to take this opportunity to settle things, for Ying's sake. She did not want to die regretting that she had left things unsaid.

Ying had an idea. As she said her prayers to the Sand Dragon, she began to dig another hole to the north of the ditch. Lan Lan was at that end, and maybe she could inch her way free into the new hole. 'Don't move,' she instructed her. 'I'm going to try and dig.'

Lan Lan smiled sadly. She wasn't about to protest. She knew that, whether or not it worked, this was the only thing they could try.

'There's something I need to tell you,' she said.

11

'Ying,' she began, 'I've wronged two people in this life, and one of them is you. I know my divorce caused you a lot of grief. I understand why. I know it hurt you. I'm a woman too. The person who understands a woman best is always another woman. Ying, I only did it because I couldn't take any more of your elder brother's beatings. It was just that. I didn't ask for love, or money, I certainly wasn't idealistic, I just imagined living like an animal. That's right, I never asked for more than that. I always envied the pigs, even though they got butchered in the end, but then that happens to all of us, doesn't it? We have our tubes tied and have operations, and even if we don't, god deals the final blow and there's no escaping that. So, I envied the pigs. And a human who envies a pig must be living a pretty terrible life. I envied the oxen too, even though they worked hard. After all, I wasn't working any less hard. You know, I got up at the crack of dawn, swept the yard, did the housework, cooked and worked, all the way through till darkness fell again. Three hundred and sixty five days of the year. Weeding, digging, scything. You name it, I did it. Oxen work hard, true, but there's a slack season when they don't have to do much. Look at me, you wouldn't think I was only twenty or so. I don't care about that though. I was born a peasant, so I was born to work hard. I accept that. '

'But I couldn't stand the beatings, I never could. He was crazy, the way he slapped me around, punched me and elbowed me and kneed me in the chest. But that was nothing compared to the whippings. You know, an ox would have collapsed under a thrashing like that. He whipped me for an hour at a time. You know how long an hour was? Sixty minutes, three thousand six hundred seconds. He whipped me until my body became a bloody mat. Then, you know what he did? He got handfuls of salt and rubbed it into the wound. If it got infected, he said, they'd have to fork out for medicine, but the pain of having salt rubbed in was a hundred times worse than the whipping itself. I had nightmares about being whipped. Once, when he'd lost money at cards, I only said a couple of things, but he went and got some brambles and ripped my clothes off. I know he learned that from listening to the old Gansu story-tellers. Do you remember them? There are lots of stories about young masters who got whipped with brambles. Why couldn't he have behaved like the good ones in the stories? Why did he have to learn from brutes?'

'The day after he beat me with the brambles, you came on a visit, and you pulled a bunch of thorns out, didn't you? Did you count them? I did. Four hundred and fifty one. That was the day I vowed that in my next life, I'd shoot him with a gun or with an arrow, four hundred and fifty one times. Yes, really. Don't be angry. I really did want to do that.'

'Don't cry. Please don't cry. If you cry, I'll stop talking. And if I keep it all inside, it'll just fester. I never dared say anything before, you know, there are people who not only don't feel sorry for you, they laugh at you. I remember there was an old woman in the village who used to threaten her daughter-in-law that if she didn't stop being so pig-headed, she'd end up like me in her next life. When I heard that, it was like a slap in the face. So I couldn't tell anyone. I just gritted my teeth and took it. I suffered terribly. My mum and dad knew I was getting beatings, but they never knew how badly. It would have broken my mother's heart if she'd known. They'd had a hard enough life as it was. I didn't want to rub salt in the wounds. Don't you agree?'

'Let's not talk about it any more. When you cry, it makes me feel bad. I never wanted to hurt you. So, no more about that. I just wanted you to know that when I went for a divorce, it was because of the beatings. If I hadn't, I would have taken my own life, either with a knife, or a rope, or with pesticides. I remember once I slung a rope over a beam and was about to put my head in the noose, but your dad saved me. And I heard that drinking pesticides was a very painful way to go. Never mind the pain, but it took so long. When would there be an end to the suffering?'

'Then my brother died. So I thought, I can't die. My mum and dad cried so much when he died, I didn't want them to cry over me too. Divorce was the only way out. Don't cry, I don't want you to suffer, I just want you to understand that I had to get a divorce because I couldn't go on. If I'd been able to put up with being beaten like that, then I would have gritted my teeth and carried on. After all, it's only a life, right? One way or another, we have to die, whether we put up a fight, or knuckle under. When I thought about it, I finally understood why people who were beaten up in the Cultural Revolution, committed suicide. People are not born to be beaten. And we're all flesh and blood, even the most heroic of us.'

'I'm a woman who knows her place. I've got no ambitions. I've never been idealistic. I just wanted peace and quiet, to be allowed to get on with my life. That's all people want to do, isn't it? Just to get on with life?'

'Of course, when my child died, I was heart-broken. I felt like the sky had fallen in. I understood how my mum and dad felt when they lost my brother. I could hardly bear to think about it. But, you know, pain, any kind of pain, goes numb with time. It just takes time and I finally got over it. People thought that that was why I wanted a divorce. It's true that is what I said. But the real reason was that I couldn't take being beaten any more. You've probably never been beaten but, believe me, it was just too much. So the people I most admire are not saints like Buddha or Guan Yin but martyrs who were tortured. If it was me, I know I couldn't stand more than a few blows before I betrayed my fellows, no matter how much I believed in the cause.'

'Don't cry.'

'So, my baby died, and in the end I fought my way back from the brink. No amount of crying would bring her back, I knew that. She died and that's that. It was her fate. But being beaten like that, when I thought of it, I felt numb, so I made a vow that I'd never hit anyone, ever. I used to slap my child every now and then, but I regret that bitterly. It's like a knife turning in my heart when I remember. So I vowed I'd never hit anyone. When I got beaten, it hurt me. When I slapped her, it hurt her too. Humans are not born to be beaten by other humans.'

'OK, don't cry any more. I've finished now.'

'I'm just happy that you know. For a very long time, I dreaded being awake, because whenever I was awake, I couldn't stop thinking about that. But I was afraid of sleeping too, because any time when I was asleep, I might hear the whip whooshing down on me. Sometimes it was real and sometimes just a dream. For a long time, I couldn't tell the difference between being awake and dreaming. He could beat me any time. On the days that he just punched and slapped me instead of whipping me, it seemed strange. In fact, it felt like he was doing me a huge favour. You know, even though being punched and slapped hurts, it's a kind of blunt pain, but the whip, that's a sharp pain, a hundred times worse than a knife. You remember that black-and-white cow we had, he whipped her until she couldn't walk any more. Just one beating and she couldn't walk. Big yellow tears oozed from her eyes. But I got whipped over and over. He would twist his torso, and take a swing with his arm, and the whiplash would go flying. One blow and I was down on the ground in the courtyard.'

'I was beaten into a state of terror. '

'Don't laugh at me. I couldn't help it. I never asked to be born a feeble woman. I just want you to understand, that's all.'

'Don't dig so fast, there's no hurry. And be careful you don't scrape your fingers. Scoop the sand, don't use your fingertips, the skin's too thin. Scoop it out your palms, yes, like that.'

'I feel so much better now I've said all this.'

12

'If I get buried by the sand, please don't cry. Tears are a waste of water, and you need water to survive. If you don't know where you are, don't run around in circles, keep going east. Forget the saltpans, your survival comes first. This fine-sand area is a long strip, narrow east-west, and long, north-south. If you go the wrong way, you'll never get out of the desert. So just head east. And whatever you do, don't walk in the heat of the day, or in no time at all, you'll be a dried-up corpse. It's best to walk at night. Look for the Big Dipper and keep it over your left shoulder all the time. Only use the torch when you absolutely have to. Don't throw the gun away, and don't let the powder get wet. If it does get wet, then make sure you dry it in the sunshine and it'll be OK. It's easy to load the gun, just take a handful of powder, not too much at a time, and pour it through the funnel into the barrel. Poke it down, half a dozen times, but don't pack it down too tight or the barrel might explode. Then you put in the shot, and if you run out, you can use some pebbles, but not too big. About the same size as the shot. Then add another half-handful of powder and tamp it down, that's to stop the shot coming out. Then get the primer out and put it on the firing pin. You're aiming for an elderly rabbit. If it's a gazelle, don't fire. The ball bearings are in a bag slung over the camel. It's a waste of powder using shot on gazelles. If you get close to it, you might wound it. But even if it's wounded quite badly, you'll never catch it. And don't waste your energy. You've got to conserve your energy. Suppose you run after a goat you've wounded and after an hour, you do catch it...you'll just be dead tired. So stick to rabbits. If you're lucky, you'll get one every time you fire. Get as close to them as you can, less than ten metres if you can.'

'Don't bother with scooping out any more sand. Look at all that's left, you haven't even got half of it out.'

'Once you catch a rabbit, drink its blood first. It doesn't matter whether it tastes nice or not. What's important is for you to survive. The blood tastes pretty foul but it's full of nutrients, and water too. If you can just catch a few rabbits and avoid getting lost, you'll get out of the desert and into the Mongols' territory. Once you've found people, they'll give you food and drink. But don't eat too much at once. They'll help you. '

'The thing to remember is only to walk at night. Or early morning. You absolutely mustn't walk in the heat of the day. When the sun is high in the sky, find a north-facing slope and dig yourself a hole. Not too deep, just go down until you get to moisture. If you find reed rhizomes, don't be greedy like I was. Just take a few. And don't make the edges of the hole too steep, or they'll fall in and you'll end up buried alive. When you get to wet sand, lie down on your front and breathe in the dampness. Take really deep breaths. Try to imagine yourself taking that dampness and the energy of the earth right into your body. It doesn't matter how much you want a drink, if you breathe the damp for an hour, you'll feel much better. And once you feel better, don't get out of the hole, lie there on your stomach for the rest of the day. That way, the sun won't dry you out. Breathing damp air is the only way to avoid getting burnt up by the sun. When it gets dark and the dew falls, then you can get up and start walking. Pick a bit of desert rice if you can find some. It's prickly, but don't worry about that. If you want to survive, you've got to expect pain. Of course, the grains are only the size of sparrows' eyes, but they're still food. Once you're in your ditch, you crack them and eat them like melon seeds. Remember, whatever happens, don't be afraid. Fear kills. Once you start to be afraid, it gets worse, it creeps up on you, little by little. It's a seed that germinates and blossoms and sets seed again. Eventually it becomes a smothering black cloud, or a great flood that drowns you. You'll lose the will to struggle on and you'll just give up and let yourself die. You'll die because your mind died first. Once your mind dies, you're dead.'

'Remember, when it comes to surviving or whatever it is, you just have to keep on walking, walking, walking. Never stop walking for one minute, and eventually you'll get where you want to go. All you need to do is go the right way, find a rabbit, and kill it. But don't chase it, whatever you do, because it will take you in the wrong direction and you'll waste energy getting back on course. As for gazelles, forget them. You've got to understand that unless you have enough powder and ball-bearings, it's just greedy to want gazelle meat. And don't let yourself be led astray by mirages. Remember, the desert is like life, it's harsh. Don't expect miracles. All you need to do is keep walking and walking and walking in the direction you've fixed on. If you're determined, you'll definitely get there. Definitely.'

'Right now, your worst enemy isn't the desert, it's yourself. You're your own worst enemy when you tell yourself to accept your fate! You can tell yourself you'll never get out of here. You can think your goal is far, far away on the horizon, when actually it's really close. You can start thinking about stuff other than walking, and those thoughts can tie you up in knots. Don't look at me like that. My guru told me that. You know who I mean, the Living Buddha who teaches me the way of Vajravarahi.'

'There's no more perfect teaching than that in the whole world.'

'Right, I should get a grip on myself too. Don't bother with scooping the sand from my chest. Get my hand out first. Look at me. I'm telling you, never lose faith. I was about ready to give up. Now I'm going to try too. I might just make more sand fall in but, after all, I'm buried already. The worst that can happen is that I get buried a bit deeper. '

'That's right, try to get my arm out first.'

13

Ying's hands were bleeding from scooping sand, but she kept on regardless. She wouldn't mind if she took all the skin off her palms if only she could save Lan Lan, she thought. Lan Lan's words had shocked and distressed her. People were strange. They had lived cheek by jowl for so many years, and today was the first time she had really understood her. She wouldn't say anything now, she thought, just concentrate on saving her. If Lan Lan was really buried alive, then she'd bury herself alongside her. She didn't want to leave her alone in the desert.

Her efforts were paying off. She had dug out a deep channel on the north side of the ditch. And, while sand continued to trickle down from time to time, Lan Lan's chest was clear of sand. If she could dig a bit more and get rid of all the sand that was pressing down on Lan Lan's top half, then the two of them could work together and pull her legs out.

Lan Lan pulled her arms free. Then she started flicking the sand off her chest, very carefully, because there was a continuing trickle of sand behind her. Luckily the moist sand was firmer, and kept its shape, so the walls held up. Also, they were on a north-facing slope and the sand was compacted. If they had been on the soft, floating sand of a south-facing slope, Lan Lan would have been done for.

Ying's head was swimming. Her efforts had made her sweat profusely and she was dehydrated. Her vision was blurred and she felt like she had a hedgehog in her throat. But she was elated because there was some hope that she could save Lan Lan. Saving her was a long way from them both getting out alive, of course, but together they had stood up to their fate and confronted it. Once you had done that, just once, you were a grown-up. Like Monk Tang on his journey to the West to fetch the Buddhist scriptures, you would only get your true reward when you had overcome eighty-one obstacles.

Ying's fingers were bleeding and she had cut her fingernails before setting off, so there was nothing to protect the pads of her fingers from the sand grains. But she didn't care if she rubbed her fingers to the bone. She dug and dug-and her fingers soon started to bleed. Lan Lan told her to scoop instead and, though it was slower work, her channel was gradually getting deeper.

Ying felt that she was saving herself just as much as Lan Lan. She was in dire straits too, but now she felt as if she was extricating herself. Often, when you save someone else, you're saving yourself.

The sun started to decline towards the west. That meant they'd been stuck here nearly three hours. They were overwhelmed with hunger and thirst. Ying felt she was going to keel over in a dead faint. After the previous night's stand-off with the dholes, they were both mentally exhausted, and physically they were living on borrowed time too. Ying just wanted to sleep. She was digging while falling asleep. That was what happened to people who died of thirst, although she did not know that. And if she fell properly asleep, the sun would extract every drop of moisture form her body and she would be set on the path to the netherworld like a sleep-walker.

'That's enough!' said Lan Lan. Ying stopped scooping sand. Lan Lan told her to shift backwards a little. They could see that there was less sand pinning Lan Lan's chest. It was only the fear that more sand would fall into the hole that stopped Lan Lan from fighting her own way out. She told Ying to move back and she gripped Ying's hands. She needed to get out in one quick jerk because that jerk would bring the sand walls down for sure. She needed to be out of there in the instant before the accumulated energy of all those sand grains roared into action. Otherwise, the sand-slip would bury her again. All their previous efforts would have been wasted but, worse still, the new sand-slip would bury her head and that would be the end of her.

They each prayed, Lan Lan to Vajravarahi, and Ying to the Sand Dragon. Then Lan Lan told Ying to dig her feet in, and she shouted: 'One, two, three…' They both heaved. The sand, of course, began to slide in with a huge momentum, but just then Lan Lan managed to kick both her legs free. With a combined strength they didn't know they had, they rolled down into the gully. The sand-slip roared into the hole and, in the blink of an eye, filled the space where Lan Lan had been trapped.

Lan Lan and Ying stood stupefied, clutching each other as tears ran down their faces.

The gully echoed with the noise of loud sobbing.

14

They ate half the reed rhizomes in the plastic bag. They had almost given their lives for those rhizomes, and they tasted like the most delicious food they had ever had. You'd find them heavenly too, I'm quite sure, if you had spent a day on the fine-sand under the blazing sun and your throat was parched. Just one nibble and the sweet nectar of the root seeps into your soul. Nectar of the gods, or of Buddha, if you're a believer. Just one drop on your tongue and all your sufferings melt away.

At the start, Ying could think of nothing but rescuing Lan Lan. Nothing else entered her head, not hunger, not thirst…Now, as the reed rhizome sap slid down into her belly, her senses re-awakened. Her belly went into spasms. It felt exactly as if an invisible hand was kneading it. She cursed the runaway camel. When she borrowed the camel in the village, she had chosen that one because it seemed good-tempered. She could not have known that it would leave them in the lurch. The wretched creature.

'The undeserving lived and the deserving died,' she thought.

Then she thought it was not surprising the camel had been terrified, when they were besieged by the dhole pack. She had been, too. The fear, which had faded as she dug, crept back along with her appalling hunger. She could hardly believe she had had such a desperate hand-to-hand fight with the beasts. It felt like a dream. Everything felt like a dream. Just now, although hunger and thirst grated on every nerve of her body, she still seemed stuck in a dream.

The sun burned down. 'Let's go,' said Lan Lan. 'Let's find a north-facing dune, dig a hole and wait till sunset.' Ying felt some trepidation at the idea of digging another hole, but she knew they would get heatstroke if they stayed out in the blazing sun. They couldn't allow the little water they had accumulated in their bodies to be licked dry by the sun. So between them they chose a good spot and began to dig. This time they knew what they were doing, so they made the hole as big as they could but not too deep. Once they detected moisture, they both crawled in. No one was worrying today about catching cold from sleeping on wet sand. Ying felt herself invaded by a strange, unreal somnolence and, in spite of herself, she fell asleep.

When she woke up, the sun was hanging over the western hills and the clouds were sunset-red. Tomorrow would be hot again. That didn't stop Ying hoping for rain though. She felt dirty and sticky, as well as thirsty. How wonderful it would be to strip off and stand naked in the middle of a cloudburst.

Lan Lan was still asleep. The powder bag and the gun lay on the edge of the hole, and Ying felt comforted. She was too tired to think of anything even though she knew they were not out of danger. There was no point in thinking, she knew that. They had no food, and thinking about it wouldn't summon it up. The same went for water. Too much thinking just made for worries, and worries took away their faith. One step at a time, she thought, one step at a time. If they got out alive, then fine. If they didn't, then that was that.

They were simply no match for the sun or for a hostile fate. But they would do what they had to do, and they would keep their dignity. Except when they got Lan Lan out of the sand, she was not one for crying nowadays. There had been a time when she burst into tears at the slightest provocation. She had made progress-she knew crying didn't change anything, life was life. Life was pressing on towards an oasis, life was looking your existence straight in the eye. There was nothing for it, if you refused to grow up, life would do what it wanted and there was nothing you could do about it.

Suddenly, something moved under some scrub nearby. It looked like a dhole. Her heart began to pound. She wanted to wake Lan Lan but thought perhaps she was seeing things. She slowly reached for the gun and only breathed more freely when she had it firmly in her grasp. But the thing under the scrub had disappeared. What a bag of nerves she was! Once bitten, twice shy. She peered around, but could not see any dholes. She heaved a sigh of relief, but then saw something move under the bit of scrub again. Anxious again, she reached for the primer and pressed it onto the firing pin. What was there to be afraid of? she asked herself, if it was a dhole? She could see a little sand whorl and then, when she looked closer, a dun-coloured rabbit.

This was a gift from the gods. Slowly, she took aim at the bush. She remembered Lan Lan saying that, at a certain distance, the pellets sprayed out like a cartwheel. She could shoot a rabbit, she was sure. The key things were to get the sights properly aligned and keep the gun still. All the same, it was the first time she had fired a gun, and her heart was in her mouth.

Maybe she should wake up Lan Lan, and get her to fire. But the desire to wake Lan Lan to the splendid sight of a rabbit she had killed herself was stronger. Her excitement overcame her fear of the gun. She could see the brown dot moving to and fro in the sights, with every breath she took. She held her breath and aimed the gun with great care. Her heart felt like it was going to burst from her chest. She pressed hard down on the trigger, only to realise that she had been pressing the metal rim instead. She could not help smiling. OK, she thought, I'll wake Lan Lan.

Lan Lan was sprawled flat out in their hole, her face covered with sand. Ying prodded her but she just carried on snoring. She's dead tired, thought Ying, and hadn't the heart to wake her. I'm so useless, she said to herself, I can't even fire a gun. Her annoyance somehow gave her confidence and she held her breath again and peered at the still-moving brown dot. She fired, feeling the stock crash into her shoulder. The noise deafened her for a moment. She didn't see any flame but she thought the gun had gone off.

Lan Lan hauled herself upright. 'What's up?' she said. 'Is it dholes?' 'I've hit a rabbit!' shouted Ying. She threw down the gun, crawled out of the hole and rushed over to the scrub. But before she got there, something brown shot away and up a distant dune.

Lan Lan followed her, half-laughing, half-crying. 'You're hopeless!' she said. 'It's much too far away!'

Ying flopped down on the sand, disappointed. She had forgotten all about the distance. She wished she hadn't fired. I really should have woken up Lan Lan, she thought. If they had shot a rabbit, even if they died from heatstroke afterwards, it would have been a happy death.

Lan Lan thought it was a pity too, but she just said: 'Forget it. The rabbit was never going to sit and wait for you to take aim and fire. Don't blame yourself. The one that got away wasn't meant for you.'

After a while, Ying pulled herself together. Lan Lan was right. Blame was pointless. The rabbit was gone. At least she had been brave enough to fire, and that was something.

'You watch carefully, I'm going to load the gun,' she told Lan Lan. So Lan Lan taught her the essentials-how to load, how to take aim, and how to fire.

15

By dusk, the sands had cooled. They ate the remaining reed rhizomes. They still had a few buns dropped from the camel, but the desert wind had made them so dry that they could not swallow them without water.

Lan Lan decided they should walk by night, and walk east, even though the saltpans were to the north of them. Just now, they needed to reach human habitation. First they need to get out alive, then they could work out how to get to the saltpans. There was a lot of work going there, or so they had heard. With the loss of their family's camel, Lan Lan could not face her parents. If only they could get to the saltpans, she could scratch together some money, at least enough to buy two more camels and take them home. Their faces fell as they talked about it. When they set off on this journey, their idea had been to make something of their lives. But what they wanted and what fate decreed were two separate things. They had not only not earned a cent, they had lost two camels. Ying was bitter. At today's prices, it would cost at least 5,000 or 6,000 yuan to replace them. That was more than half what her brother Bai Fu needed to get himself a new wife. Lan Lan sighed heavily then, looked at Ying's despondent face, and tried to comfort her. 'Stop thinking about it. The dead one's dead, the runaway's run away. Who knows? It might go home. So we've really only lost one camel.' Ying knew Lan Lan was right, but that was only a possibility. It was an old camel, and it knew its way around. It might try to get home, but it might meet more dholes, or wolves, or hunters. If hunters found it, it would be easy enough to catch, because it still had a rope through its nose.

'If the camel turns up at home,' said Lan Lan, 'My mum and dad will be really worried.' Ying could see it all: Her mother-in-law's weeping fit to bring the heavens down, Lan Lan's dad looking grey-faced, sitting on the edge of the *kang* bed pulling on his pipe, the villagers trying to comfort them. This was what had happened when her elder brother had died. It occurred to Ying that she had no husband to be broken-hearted if she died, and the thought needled her.

'Just stop thinking about it,' said Lan Lan. 'There's no point. It's more important to get on the road. We'll rest in a damp sand hole by day and walk by night. If we meet more dholes, then we're done for. If we can stay alive till we get to the saltpans, then we'll be fine.' Ying agreed.

Ying was exhausted and would have liked to sleep some more, even to hang around here a few days before setting off, but she kept the thought to herself. She could say anything she wanted if they came across camels, and food and water. Just now, if they did not get on their way, she would die in the fine-sand.

They made a move as soon as the sun went down behind the western mountains. As before, Lan Lan slung the gun over her shoulder and Ying carried the torch. They had used up all the energy from the rhizomes and were so hungry that their bellies gurgled. The rhizomes had just made them hungrier. They were being swept along by their hunger and thirst, especially thirst, which threatened to overwhelm them. Lan Lan's lips had gone a blueish-purple and were swollen and scabbed, because she kept licking them. She remembered her father saying that, in the fine-sand desert, you must absolutely never lick your lips, no matter how thirsty you were. That was because your saliva had toxins in it and a few licks would make them swell. Ying, always careful of her appearance, had been mindful not to lick and she told Lan Lan to stop too. But Lan Lan wouldn't listen and her lips were fully half-an-inch fatter than before. On top of that, her cheeks were sunken and her eyes were enormous, glazed and expressionless. Ying could only imagine, judging from Lan Lan's face, what she looked like herself. Her lips were not swollen, but must have gone a lot darker. She touched her face, and the skin felt dried out. This was what dehydration did to you.

Water...the thought was cooling, but it was immediately followed by an overpowering, violent thirst.

Ying rubbed her lower back and peered into the distance. The stars weren't out yet and there was a rosy after-glow above the western horizon. The dark outline of the mountains was beautiful. The wind had got up, a warm wind but still refreshing. If only they had enough to eat and drink and were here on holiday, it would be a beautiful place to be. But not right now, not when the two of them were fighting for their lives. Ying gazed numbly westwards and made herself swallow. If her lover was here, she thought, it would put him in a poetic mood. Strangely, the thought of him left her numb too. The feelings she had had before were gone. He was right, she thought, love is a feeling that doesn't last with the lack of water.

They were plodding along very slowly. They walked stiffly, and Ying thought she could hear a dry cracking in her legs. It must be her knee and ankle joints creaking, she thought. They certainly hurt. She remembered what her mother always said: 'Slowly does it. Just keep moving.' She made herself believe that with each step they were getting nearer. Probably Lan Lan was doing the same, but her body swayed as if it was refusing to obey her. The slope they were climbing was taking them a very long time. Looking at the mountains not far ahead of them, Ying felt a pang of fear.

At the top of the slope, Lan Lan flopped down in the sand, and Ying stretched out on her back. It was dark, the wind was cool and the air held a hint of moisture. This was why it was good to be walking at night. But although they had the will-power, their bodies would not obey them. Like cars, they needed fuel. No cars could run without fuel. It was all very well to rest on damp sand by day and walk by night, but it needed strong, healthy bodies to do that, and well-fed and watered ones. The rhizomes had only provided them with a little nutrition, enough to keep them alive for the time being. To get up and over the mountain ahead of them, to cross this vast desert, seemed impossible.

Ying drooped beside Lan Lan. On the sand hills, the wind was a lot colder. 'We should go,' said Lan Lan. 'Don't fall asleep here, or you'll die.' 'Yes,' said Ying. 'Come on,' said Lan Lan. 'OK,' said Ying. But neither of them moved. Ying sighed, and pillowed her head on Lan Lan's belly.

Ying's body seemed to have lost all its bone marrow, nerves and blood. How she longed to sleep. 'Get up,' said Lan Lan. 'There's only another eighty *li* (500m) of desert to the east of us. I think we've done more than half of it. There'll be herders on the other side.' 'Get up,' repeated Ying. And they did. Leaning on each other, they followed the ridge of the dune eastwards.

Ying was so consumed with thirst that it took a while for her to feel her legs. Then the shooting pains began, through the soles of her feet and up her calves. Apart from a few trips to gather desert rice, she had spent very little time in the fine-sand and the walking was hard. It was the same for Lan Lan but she, at least, had done all the hard labour in her husband's family and was much stronger and fitter than Ying. Still, carrying the gun was tiring, even though it only weighed about ten pounds. As they walked along, it seemed like a rapacious beast consuming her energy. As to Ying, even the torch felt like a lead weight.

It was very dark, but that did not matter, because they had the Big Dipper to guide them. Its brightness would keep the hobgoblins of the night at bay. In fact, it was as reassuring as their gun. But their thirst was getting more intense, clouding not just their judgement but their eyes. Their eyeballs felt rough, and they could hear them rasping as they moved. Their joints creaked more with each step, at least, that was how it sounded in the silence of the night. That had never happened to them before.

In spite of the pain, they plodded on, their hopes rising with each step. In her confused state, Ying imagined herself walking towards Ling Guan. He almost seemed to be standing far away in the darkness, waving at her. The thought gave her strength. It was very strange. Even though she knew she was imagining things, the strength that it gave her was real enough. She tried to sharpen the image. Seeing him meant something, she was sure. It was not just accidental. Maybe he was really there, out there in the night in the east, keeping watch over his flocks. It was quite possible. He had told her how much he liked horse-riding. She could see him riding a horse in her mind's eye, although she had never seen him on horse- back in reality, so in her mind, he was bouncing around as if he was on a camel. Whatever beast he was riding on, it really didn't matter, even if it was a sheep, just so long as he was there. Ying cheered up. She had a mind to tell Lan Lan, because she looked completely done in, but then thought that baby Flower could not possibly be in the pastures. In any case, she had heard Lan Lan say that Flower was not as present in her heart as she used to be. No visualizing could cure Lan Lan's exhaustion.

Her vision enabled Ying to walk much faster, even though her legs hurt, even though she was so parched that every pore seemed to be screaming. It gave meaning to her walking, and everything seemed to be much easier to bear. How strange. Ying was amused.

16

But her renewed energy did not last. Not long after midnight, Ying found she could not walk any more. Every time they toiled up a slope, she only made it with Lan Lan's help. She felt light-headed. Lan Lan was using the gun stock as a walking stick. She wanted Ying to have it, but Ying had no strength even to pick it up. Eventually, the pair of them helped each other along, Lan Lan leaning on the gun stock and Ying leaning on Lan Lan. They got to the top of a gentle slope and collapsed on the sand, defeated by hunger and thirst.

'I can't go any further,' said Ying, panting, 'Let me die here.' Her throat was too dry to get the words out, but Lan Lan knew what she was trying to say. She said nothing in reply. She knew that death was coming closer, as remorselessly as the coffins that bore the bodies of the dead from the village. Even if the sun were not scorching the following day, their thirst would do for them. Their last drink of water was a long time ago. Since then, they had only had the few drops of reed rhizome sap. Lan Lan remembered how happy they had been, digging up the rhizomes. They had been a lifeline, one that would get them out of here. But those rhizomes had cost them so much risk and effort to dig up, and the liquid from them was a drop in the ocean compared to their overwhelming need to eat and drink. She did not dare think what fate awaited them tomorrow when the sun blazed overhead once more.

Ying felt that she was going to die. Life had become a candle in the wind, a little, wavering flame that could be extinguished at any moment. Her heartbeat sounded weak, as if it might stop at any minute. People said that life was just a breath that could be snuffed out just like that, and now she was experiencing this for real. As soon as that slender, thread-like breath was cut off by the wind, there would be one more lonely soul to wander the fine-sand. According to Blackie, the ghosts of people who died far from home were never at peace. Without the King of the Underworld to take them back to Hell, the ghosts were left weeping over a pile of desiccated bones. Only when the bones were buried were these souls laid to rest. Her head suddenly teemed with stories about death that she had heard in the village. What would she turn into when she died, she wondered? She did not want to be reincarnated as a human, it was too much trouble. She would like to be a bird in her next life, best of all a skylark, singing all day in the trees. Even a fox would be all right. Ying, like Lan Lan, liked foxes. There was something magical about these quick, agile creatures. They were fleeting, like the wind, leaving as little trace behind them as plum blossom. She would really like to be re-born as a fox that worshipped the moon. She would raise her muzzle to the moon, and cultivate her moon worship until she passed into fairy form. She would go and haunt that bookworm, Ling Guan. He would be old by then, but she didn't care, it would still be Ling Guan. She could even vomit up a rare elixir for him, and make him eat it so that he would regain his youth. By that time, everyone would have forgotten them and she could come and go as she pleased with complete invisibility. No one could force her to marry, and Poxy Xu would not disgust her ever again. If need be, she could give birth to a whole litter of fairy foxes, all named Ling Guan: Ling Guan the Elder, Ling Guan the Second, Ling Guan the Third, and so on…She could not help laughing at the comical thought of a litter of sharp-muzzled little Ling Guans. They would play in the sand dunes, sing and fight, and worship the moon, running around, as fleeting as the wind. Their footsteps would stir up eddies of sand and leave prints like plum blossom all over the dunes. The best painters could not paint plum blossom like that. These creatures were so elegantly free and easy, they were heaven-inspired, in earthly form.

Her thirst reminded her that her life was drawing to a close. She felt she would not live to see the sun rise. She wasn't particularly bothered now. Death had seemed such a big thing, but now it was just like dropping off to sleep. Once you had done what you had to do, and really gone to sleep, then there was little more to it. She thought of Pan Pan. How strange that, here in the desert, this was the first time she had thought of Pan Pan. It told her that she trusted her mother-in-law to look after him. Even if Pan Pan lost his mother, he would not be ill-treated. Ying was quite clear about that. She also felt she should never have become a mother. She had never felt for her child the kind of stubborn attachment that she had for Ling Guan. She could not help it. Everything she felt was overshadowed by her lover. They only mattered because they were Ling Guan's family, his baby, his relatives, his parents and so on. It was too bad, and it was not fair, but there was nothing to be done about it. She hadn't wanted it that way, it just felt like it had always been like that.

She was so light-headed by this time that her child was only a vague image too. She was breathing shallowly and her heartbeat was weak. Let me die, she thought. However long you lived, you had to die eventually. Only she did not want to turn into a thirst-ridden ghost. In the village, the ghosts of those who had died of thirst always came to tickle people and the person being tickled used to cry out with thirst. Even if you gave them three bowlfuls of water, they were still thirsty. They would have to call a shaman, who would make cuts on the forehead of the afflicted person. Once the malevolence had been cut out, the shaman would lash the ghost with a whip. It was said that the imprint on the subconscious of those who died of hunger and thirst was so deep that they could never rid themselves of their craving for food and water. They would wail all night long in a desperate search for water, and when they found it, it would turn into pus or blood, or live embers. This was a thirst that could never be slaked. Ying did not want to become that kind of ghost. She just wanted to die, cleansed in body and soul. Of course, the sun would cover her lips with dark scabs but her heart would be pure. Please god, let me be re-born as a fox, she thought.

With difficulty, she made her eyes swivel and search the darkness. Her eyeballs felt as dry as cart axles that had not been greased in years. The stars seemed to be rustling in the sky, as if they were quarrelling. They crackled with the same noise her knee joints made as she walked, the noise that soybeans made when you fried them. What a racket the stars made. What a strange world it was.

The night drew on and, after a long time, the darkness seemed to pale. They could make out the vague, mysterious outlines of the dunes. The drowsiness that comes before death once more enveloped her. The viscosity of her blood had become a noose, and her heart, starved of nutrients, felt unbearably heavy, incapable of pushing the sludge-like blood platelets around her body. If she went to sleep, she thought, when she woke up, she would have turned into a wisp of smoke. Then her soul would blow around in the air above the desert, like the wind.

She remembered the stories her mum used to tell her about the 'Ghost of Impermanence'. These spirits were sent to fetch the spirits of the dead to the Underworld. When Han Tou, her husband, was dying but still clinging on to life, her mum used to say it was because Ling Guan was beside him and the Ghosts of Impermanence couldn't get near enough to snatch the soul away. Her mum said that a young person's energy leaked a lot, and to the Ghost he was a fire they couldn't get close to. As soon as Ling Guan left, Han Tou breathed his last. Her mother's words spooked Ying so much that the hairs stood up on the back of her neck. Was there a Ghost of Impermanence standing by her now, Ying wondered, waiting to snatch her soul away? Lan Lan gave a snore. Ying realised she was afraid, not of death but of ghosts, even though she would become a ghost herself when she died. She dared not turn around and look behind her, in case she caught sight of a Ghost of Impermanence. She had seen them in the theatre, with their deathly pale faces and tall thin figures, wearing pointy hats. If she saw one of those, she would be frightened to death, and the Guards would have no trouble in snatching her soul.

Her terror had banished sleep. Then she really did hear a footstep behind her. It must surely be a ghost. How could it be anything else in this godforsaken place? Her heart began to race. This was the heart that had beaten so sluggishly just a few moments before. Very strange. The sound of footsteps had to come from a poltergeist. The grain mill in the village had one of those. It used to bang whenever someone entered the mill at night, and would keep up the disturbance until cockcrow. Absorbed in her thoughts, Ying even forgot her thirst. Her scalp tingled. Something came closer until it was right behind her. She could hear breathing, a hoarse panting. She nearly screamed, but didn't want to scare herself even more.

Ying sensed the ghost reach out its claws. It was going to pinch her neck. When she was little, her mum used to say that ghosts pinched you. She used to recite: 'A headache comes from a fever. A bellyache comes from constipation. A gut ache comes from the pinch of a ghost.' She really did feel a hot breath on her neck. Then she thought, what am I afraid of? It's only death. And I need to see what this ghost looks like. Torch in hand, she whirled around.

A grotesquely-shaped black shadow loomed in front of her.

She quickly turned the torch on and gave a loud cry.

17

It was the camel.

She prodded Lan Lan, and shouted: 'The camel! The camel!'
Lan Lan crawled to her feet. The camel stood there snorting. This
was marvellous. They had both given up on ever finding the camel,
assuming it had run away for good. Lan Lan stumbled over to the
beast, loosened the rope around the pack and pulled off the plastic
flagon. It was still more than half full of water. 'Water! Water!'
cried Ying. Even the word sounded refreshing. Lan Lan unscrewed
the top and passed it to Ying. 'Don't drink too much,' she warned.
'Just a little. If you drink too much, your stomach will burst.' Ying
obediently took just a mouthful, and swallowed a little at a time. Far
from being refreshing, it burned like fire. Her oesophagus must have
a crack in it, she thought. She struggled to get a couple of mouthfuls
down, but felt more thirsty than ever.

Lan Lan took the flagon off her and wouldn't let her drink any
more. In the village, she had seen thirsty people die from drinking
too much too quickly, because their stomachs had shrunk.

Lan Lan took a sip herself, then shone the torch on the camel. It
seemed to have lost a lot of their belongings. The flour bag hung in
tatters and there was no flour left. There were a couple of holes in
the goatskin bag, so there was no water in that either. Luckily, the

flagon was undamaged. The cloth wrapped around the buns was still there and there were two dry buns left. There had been over a dozen. The rest must have been jolted out into the fine-sand.

The sleeping mat was still tied to the packsaddle, luckily. The canvas bag of ball bearings was intact, together with a bag of gunpowder and a ball of twine. It was too bad the goatskin bag had been damaged and lost all its water, though.

The camel had trodden on its rope and broken it. There was only a metre or so left. Lan Lan got the twine, twisted it into cord and extended the rope. They were both astonished that the camel had actually come back. Old Shun, Lan Lan's dad, had always told them that camels had a sense of smell so keen that, even when facing into the wind, it could distinguish smells from ten *li* away. It would have had no trouble in finding them once it made up its mind. In the meantime, it must have been able to feed itself, as it had hardly lost weight.

Why the camel had changed its mind after running away was a mystery. It was obvious why it wanted to get away from the dholes and the heat. You could hazard a guess that it had come back because it couldn't bear to abandon two women in the desert, or something like that. But it must have had a desperate struggle with its conscience to make that decision, as desperate as a battle with the dholes.

Ying felt contrite as she grasped the rope. It couldn't have been easy for the camel to escape in the first place. Now it was back, of its own accord, and the first thing they did to it was hang onto the rope. It showed they still didn't trust it. Did it feel hurt? Ying wondered. She shone the torch into the camel's eyes and saw they still had a kindly, gentle look in them. It was not ashamed of having run away, nor was it delighted to be caught again. It was simply calm and indifferent.

They sipped the water and nibbled a few mouthfuls of bun, but just felt more hungry. Still, they did not dare eat more. They did not want to die with swollen bellies. That would be as bad as starving to death.

With the camel back, fatigue overwhelmed them again. Lan Lan ordered the beast to kneel and they propped themselves against its flanks and took a nap. Not for long, but they slept soundly all the same.

When they woke up, it was broad daylight. They chewed a couple of mouthfuls of bun to keep them going. Now that they had the camel, Lan Lan suggested that they stop walking east and turn north instead. That was where the saltpans were and if they kept on walking, they couldn't miss them. If they carried on eastwards, they would still have to turn north and would have wasted even more time.

Unwittingly, she was leading them straight into the trackless Gobi Desert, where their lives would once more hang in the balance.

The sun was up in the east and the sky was stained with pink. The gully bottom was still in deep shadow, and the contrast with the sun's rays was as sharp as the lines in a woodcut. The dunes billowed away into the distance where they merged with the sandy mountains. Nearer to them, the sand rippled like waves of the sea, so perfect it seemed a shame to tread on it.

There was a fresh desert wind. Ying shivered, and huddled in her bright blue cotton jacket. Lan Lan looked whey-faced and was goose-pimpled with cold. It was the chill of the desert dawn that had woken them after just a few hours. They had been too tired to unpack all the bedding. Well, they had better get on the road while it was still cool. How extreme the climate was in the fine-sand, thought Ying, like a freezer in the morning but a furnace by noon.

They settled between the camel's humps. A camel's back was warm and sturdy, and they felt as if they had crawled back on deck after falling into the sea. Camels truly were the ships of the desert.

The camel rocked them as it paced along. Its slow, steady gait seemed to make the crests of the dunes sway too, and the sun which poked above the horizon. The sun's rays crept over Ying's face, bathing her with warmth. She felt like she had come back to life. It didn't matter that in a few hours the sun would be bearing down on them again. The very fact that they had the camel back made her feel everything was going to be all right. It was too bad she was just a woman. Last night's walking had given her stabbing pains in her legs and the soles of her feet. In fact, she hurt all over, from head to foot. Without the camel, she could not have moved an inch. She had no reserves of strength, at least not enough to carry her across this desert ocean. But the camel did. It was a huge, placid beast, contemplative as a philosopher. Without speaking a word, it gave an impression of strength that permeated the depths of Ying's soul.

Camels were afraid of the desert, you could tell that from the way they tossed their heads and flicked their ears. Lan Lan's dad always had to use the whip on his beasts, scoring their backs and even lashing their noses, the most sensitive part of them, before he could get them to walk on obediently. The camels knew quite well that, as soon as they were in the desert, they would be permanently saddled, either with goods or humans. They were bred as beasts of burden, it was their karma, just like Ying's was to wait. And there was not an animal in this world that suffered willingly. Ying felt a degree of respect for the camel between her thighs. You ran away, but came back of your own accord, she thought. You didn't have to, you could have pleased yourself, lying in a sheltered gully, chewing the cud, eating desert rice or fresh grass. Now you have to carry two women who are in as bad a state as you are, without knowing what the future holds.

'I've got nothing but respect for you, camel,' she thought.

Lan Lan was trying to find the track. She knew the way to the saltpans, but the confrontation with the dholes had left her completely disorientated. Looking at the billowing dunes, she felt as if fate had tossed them into the unknown. She had had to tackle the unknown many, many times since she was a girl, but it never got any easier. Her world got more unfamiliar by the day, and she did not know how to cope.

'Do you know where we're going?' asked Ying. 'I'm really confused,' Lan Lan admitted. 'It's not good. But let's start moving. So long as we're going in the right direction, we'll get there.' We'll have to, thought Ying.

As they walked, the sun rose higher in the sky and the heat grew more vicious. They had to go easy on that life-saving water, no matter how parched they both were, because they did not know where the next water would come from. The most they could allow themselves was the occasional sip, and that was when their thirst made it hard to swivel their eyeballs. 'You can't drink too much at a time,' said Lan Lan, 'it just turns into urine, and we need to make every drop of water keep us alive. We've got to have self-restraint.'

A couple of hours later, they dismounted because the camel was exhausted. It was frothing at the mouth and puffing like a bellows. 'We'd better give it a rest,' said Lan Lan. They found a bit of scrub and unsaddled it. Lan Lan was shocked to discover that the packsaddle had rubbed the animal's back red-raw. The sores must have happened when it first ran away and the saddle bounced around. The sores were hideous. Ying felt full of remorse at the thought that they had been putting all their weight on them all day.

Lan Lan got some salt from the canvas bag, mixed it with water and washed the camel's wounds, grumbling as she did so: 'Why didn't you complain? We would never have ridden you if we'd known.' The camel snorted dismissively.

The sun rose high in the sky and its scorching rays poured down on them. 'Let's do what we did before and lie in a damp hole until dark, then move on,' said Lan Lan. 'We should be OK to get to the saltpans if we go easy on the water.' Ying knew Lan Lan was trying to reassure her. If they hadn't got mixed up with the dholes, they would have reached the saltpans without any trouble at all. They could not be so sure now because they were far off course. But she said nothing. They could not afford to give in to their feelings in their present predicament. Finally she said, 'Just so long as we don't give up, we'll be fine.' Now they had the camel, she could say anything.

Lan Lan was surprised to discover half a bottle of cooking oil in one of the saddlebags. They had brought it to cook with, but she had packed it separately from the pots so it wouldn't get broken. They had ditched the pots and pans, but here was the cooking oil. It didn't taste nice, but it would nourish them because it contained more calories than the buns. 'We won't touch the oil yet,' Lan Lan decided. 'We'll eat the buns first, soaked in water because otherwise we won't be able to get them down. We'll drink the oil as a last resort.'

Just the sight of the oil seemed to cool Ying down.

They found a north-facing gully with some scrub cover and dug until they reached damp sand. They made two holes, the bigger one for the camel who, although it stored water in its body, needed shelter from the scorching rays of the sun just like they did. Its body moisture would not evaporate so fast in the hole, and it could breathe the moist air. They made sure to dig well away from steep banks this time. Lan Lan used the hunting knife to cut some of the vegetation and threw it into the camel's hole as fodder.

They were still hungry and thirsty but they felt a lot better now. Without the camel, they really had been in dire straits. Then, hunger had dug its claws into them and ripped them apart. Now, they had food and water and their tormenting thirst felt bearable. They only had buns, water and oil in small quantities to look forward to, but those things were wonderful.

From time to time, Lan Lan dissolved salt in a little water in the flagon screw-top, and washed the camel's sores. She got Ying to hold the flagon firm between her knees as she mixed it. Every time she did it, Ying felt like the flagon might suddenly leap from her grip and splatter all that life-saving water onto the sand. It was as if the air was full of mischievous hands, ready to tug the flagon from her and she gripped it so hard, her arms ached. She felt so stressed that by the time Lan Lan had finished, she was limp from exhaustion.

Lan Lan tipped the remaining salt solution into her cupped hands and offered it to the camel. The camel put out its tongue and licked up the drops. Camels loved salt and this was a small treat for good behaviour. If you worked it out, the camel was getting more water than they were, but that was fine, because no way did they want the camel's sores to get infected. They wanted them to scab over as soon as possible, so it could carry them. Even more importantly, now that they had the camel, they felt they were back on course.

18

The sisters-in-law rested by day and travelled for two more nights. That should have taken them as far as the saltpans. Instead, to their dismay, they found themselves in the vast gritty expanse of the Gobi Desert. Lan Lan cursed silently. This was really bad news. When she had been to the saltpans before, there was no sign of the Gobi. They must have gone the wrong way. They had eaten all the buns and had only a little water left. True, they hadn't touched the oil yet but, when they did, it wouldn't last long. The camel's sores had scabbed over but it was exhausted, and neither of them had the heart to ride it. They took it in turns to lead the beast, while the other got a little help by holding onto its tail. Their legs no longer felt like theirs. Later on, they took it in turns to ride and walk, for a couple of hours at a time.

The camel's humps were floppy, meaning it had used up most of its stores of food and water. There was little vegetation along the way, and although Lan Lan specially chose places with the most scrub to rest during the daytime, the humps flopped anyway. Dad always said that camels consumed their reserves only as a last resort. It was best to ensure they always had enough food and water, especially water, which they could not do without. Lan Lan remembered that, on her last trip to the saltpans, they had halted especially to allow the camels to graze and drink. This camel was short of food because they had gone the wrong way. Lan Lan took off the saddle, pulled out some of its straw stuffing and fed it to the starving camel, though it was an inadequate meal. Then she padded up the saddle again with their sleeping mat.

Camels preferred to graze at night, but at night they were marching. In theory it could graze by day, but every gully they stopped in turned into a furnace and after it had grazed a bit, the camel retreated to lie down in its hole. Besides, they couldn't always find even dried stalks. The beast was on the point of collapse.

Luckily, the sores on its back healed quickly. Camels always got sores because of the loads they carried, but they naturally formed thick, hard calluses. The salt water helped too. So long as the camel had the strength to go on, it could carry them too.

When they set off for the fine-sand, Lan Lan's dad had instructed them: 'If your camel gets too tired to walk, crumble up a bit of bun and feed it to the camel.' That was all very well, but just now they had no buns to eat themselves, let alone to feed the camel. In order to keep the beast going, they had to make halts at night too, wherever they found some withered stalks. But they were drier than the desert itself, and the camel was so short of water by now that it turned up its nose at them. People were no different. If you'd been baked by the sun for three days, you might be sniffy about fried noodles too.

When you weren't looking for a ribbon oasis, you might just find it anyway, and the fresh green plants that grew there wouldn't do any harm either to humans or camels. But when you went looking for a ribbon oasis, there was no chance of finding one. At midday, Ying thought she'd spotted a ribbon oasis and could see water and animals grazing, but Lan Lan said it was just a mirage. Sure enough, very soon the beautiful vision vanished into thin air. There was no point going to look for it, it was as elusive as flies' fart.

There was at least more for the camel to eat in the Gobi. A month of this kind of grazing, thought Lan Lan, and the camel's humps would plump up again. But they had to keep going. They weren't here to herd camels, they were on their way to find saltpans. Lan Lan tried hard to work out where they were, but she had to admit they must have missed them. The saltpans were actually an oasis, but not a big one, and if you were off course by as little as half a *li*, you might easily miss it.

What were they to do?

'We'll have to go back,' said Lan Lan. 'When we get back to the fine-sand, we'll go west. If we're lucky, we might just bump into the saltpans.'

Back in the fine-sand, they tethered the camel to a bush and walked to the top of the highest hill they could see. It was hard work climbing but once you got to the top, there was a chance that they would see in the distance the shining white strip of a saltpan. Dragging leaden legs, they toiled upwards. The climb took at least two hours and left them completely drained. Once they were at the top and had got their breath back, they looked around and were disappointed to discover that they were not on the highest peak. Waves of higher mountains, all of sand, stretched away into the distance. They were horror-struck.

'My god!' cried Ying. She slumped to the ground and said nothing more.

Lan Lan was also struck dumb. Both of them felt like crying, but no tears came. They were uncomprehending. They scoured the horizon. If only they could see any strip of white, they could crawl towards it. But there was nothing but sandy mountains. Even if they crawled all the way to the horizon, it was hard to say whether they would find any saltpans.

'Let's go down,' said Lan Lan.

'I'm not moving,' said Ying. 'I might as well die right here, on the sand mountain, and turn into a heap of bones.'

'Come on,' said Lan Lan. 'Let's go the way we planned and then we'll see.'

Looking down at the little brown dot that was the camel, Ying thought, I knew this would happen. It was not just a waste of energy to climb the mountain, it was discouraging too.

She was too tired to walk down. She found the steepest part, sat down and slid. Somehow the sliding, with the wind in her ears, as if she had grown wings, cheered her up. When the slope levelled off, she heard Lan Lan shout. 'Mind your trousers! You'll wear a hole in the seat of the trousers if you carry on sliding.'

Ying was sorry to damage her trousers, but she was having fun. What did trousers matter when they did not know whether they would live or die? She skipped and jumped down the slope, carried by sand that flowed like water. She felt invigorated, more relaxed than she had in a long time. She shouted with excitement, and the sandy gully suddenly came alive. Infected by Ying's excitement, Lan Lan stopped worrying about her trousers and began to slide too. The shouting blew away days of depression.

After a while, Ying had second thoughts. If she really did wear a hole in the seat of her trousers, it would be embarrassing when she got to the saltpans and had to face people. She turned over, and, facing downwards, began to swim down on her stomach. Her body made swishing sounds with every stroke. She got sand in her clothes, and the itching felt strangely pleasant. Lan Lan started to swim down too, and the gully echoed to their shouts. The sudden elation washed all their worries away.

At the bottom of the slope, they brushed the sand off and started to laugh. Living under other people's gaze for so many years, they had never had a chance to let off steam like this. Who would have thought that, in such dire straits, they would have started behaving like young girls again.

They celebrated their cheerful mood with a gulp of cooking oil each.

19

However, the burst of gaiety had sapped all their energy, and anxiety crept up on them again. How much further could they go? Would they ever get to the saltpans? The more they questioned, the worse they felt. They decided to put it out of their minds. The sun was no longer quite as strong and so they mounted the camel and set off towards the west. It would not necessarily lead them to the saltpans, but staying here would certainly be the death of them. Sometimes even a blind donkey could find itself some fodder, so they might bump into someone going to the saltpans, or perhaps a herder. It didn't matter who they met, all they had to do was ask the way and they'd get an answer. And if they met someone decent, they might be given a little food and water.

Towards dusk, they came across a camel skeleton next to a crescent dune. Lan Lan was delighted. This was the next best thing to meeting human beings. The most striking was the skull, whose two dark eye sockets stared blankly at the new arrivals. The skeleton was almost complete, with the teeth and ribcage intact. It did not look as if it had been ripped apart by wild animals, either before or after death. Their mount was alarmed at the sight of its dead kin, however, and flung its head, flapped its ears and snorted, nearly throwing them off its back. According to Lan Lan's dad, it was because the camel was spitting at a ghost, saliva being the thing ghosts were most afraid of. It seemed unlikely that the ghost of the dead beast still lingered next to the skeleton, although there was a superstition that some ghosts kept watching over unburied bodies, only departing when the bones were under the ground. Ying didn't believe it, but was a little scared all the same.

'Look,' said Lan Lan. 'This camel was carrying salt.' And she pointed to some fragments of a cloth bag. The camel must have belonged to a Mongolian salt trader, and died of fatigue. Ying couldn't see any evidence of salt, but she was cheered up anyway. Whatever it was, it was good. They had seen hardly any evidence of human presence, in all their travels through the fine-sand and the Gobi, but these camel bones proved that humans had come this way.

Then she wondered if it was actually a wild camel. She did not say so, for fear of puncturing Lan Lan's happiness. They needed to have hope, even if it was illusory. Hope was always better than despair.

If this camel was really on its way to the saltpans, Ying thought, then it must mean that the saltpans were not far away. In that case, their camel should be able to struggle that far. She did not want to speculate about the cause of the camel's death, because it was depressing. It was possible that there was no fresh grass and no water in the vicinity. Otherwise, why would the camel have died? Perhaps it had died of disease, not of thirst. She imagined it lying in the gully, calmly resigned to its fate, in the same way Buddhist monks died while sitting in meditation. When the knife that would sever its life was raised, perhaps it even stretched out its neck in expectation. Ying gave a long sigh, wondering what fate had in store for her.

Lan Lan ordered their camel to kneel, and they both got on. The camel lurched unsteadily to its feet. Ying looked around at the skeleton. 'Goodbye,' she said. 'You came to a sad end.' And she felt a pang of sadness at the thought that if they carried on like this, she might end up as a skeleton in the sands too.

They walked on. The track had obviously been well-used and they came across more and more bones, skulls, thigh bones and sometimes whole skeletons, sticking conspicuously out of the sand. This must be pasturage, not a camel track, Ying thought. Otherwise why so many bones? The thought was comforting.

Lan Lan was still hoping to shoot a wild rabbit, but the odd thing was that they had not seen a single living creature after the rabbit Ying put up. Even a desert rat would be something, thought Lan Lan with a sigh. She had eaten them roasted, as a child, and the flesh tasted better than chicken meat. Semi-starved as they were, Lan Lan almost wished they could see dholes again. Almost, but not quite. Actually, the memory of those sinister creatures was terrifying. But maybe they might see a lone dhole and, if she could shoot it, that would be meat for them to eat. The villagers were divided in their opinions of dhole meat: Some liked it, others said it was stringy like a fox, and still others said that it was gamey, like eating a raven. She didn't care. Meat was meat, and could keep you alive. But it was sod's law: When you didn't want to meet someone, they were everywhere, and you went looking for them, they were nowhere to be seen.

The cooking oil was wonderful. Just a mouthful gave them more calories than a meal. So meals became the oil. Once they'd started on a few 'meals', soon only half the bottle was left, even though they only took small sips. They couldn't help that. 'There must be a hungry ghost stealing our oil,' said Lan Lan. It happened a lot in their village, that if there was a hungry ghost around and you killed a fat bellwether sheep, it wouldn't last you many meals. Of course there was another saying, too: If someone ate everything you put in front of them, it told you they would always be poor. Dad always put visitors to the test this way. If they picked at the meat at dinner, then their visitor was going to be wealthy. If the meat disappeared without you seeing, then the visitor was definitely poor. According to Dad, neither Lan Lan nor Ying would ever be rich: Food and water disappeared in front of them, and that included leftovers. Ying didn't want to believe in fate, but often when things happened, she felt herself pulled one way or another by something stronger than herself. Perhaps fate did exist after all.

Finally, they came across proof that they were on a camel track. Next to one skeleton lay a packsaddle. The evidence was incontrovertible. The wooden frame was pretty much weathered by the wind. There was also a pile of ancient camel dung. Lan Lan was elated. Finally, they must be on the right road. Ying was happy too, but doubts crept in all the same. Why were there so many camel bones? The bones told them that a lot of camels had passed this way, but also that it had been a long and difficult trek, and the camels had ended their lives here. Ying could not help thinking that the same fate awaited the two of them. Did this track really lead to the saltpans? How far away were they? Could they keep going until they found water? These were all unanswerable questions. Of course Lan Lan knew this quite well. She just did not want to admit it.

Ying was most worried about the camel. They had cooking oil to give them calories, but the camel had so little that its humps had collapsed to empty skin bags. How much further could it go? After all, it was carrying two adults on its back, a combined weight of at least two hundred pounds. It was getting very unsteady when it got to its feet, and when it tottered uphill, it seemed in danger of falling. At the next hill, they got down and slogged up it, hanging onto the camel's tail. The camel seemed near the end of its strength too. Otherwise, why would the sight of those camel bones have alarmed it so much?

20

They paused and drank a mouthful of the cooking oil. They would walk at night again. The camel bones were like an eerie forest at night but at least they knew they were still on the track. Ying was afraid that, otherwise, they would be stumbling around as blind as headless flies. As Lan Lan said, 'Slowly does it. Just keep walking.' Every step took them nearer their goal.

They ordered the camel to kneel.

The camel hesitated a moment before slowly going down. Lan Lan sighed. The beast was so tired. They got on and Lan Lan shook the rope, and shouted at it to stand. The camel swayed and struggled to get to its feet. Finally, it got its front feet up, then sagged to the ground again. It groaned, then tried again to stagger its feet. 'I'll get off, you ride,' said Lan Lan. She shouted and tried to pull the camel up by its tail, but it only gave a great sigh and lay still.

'It just wasn't up to it,' thought Ying, and she got off too. The camel's nostrils were flared and it was breathing heavily. There were dried-up stalks on the hillocks around them, but the camel did not look at them. It was too thirsty, its throat too parched, to swallow the sun-shrivelled stalks. Ying felt immensely grateful to it for bringing them this far. Where would they have ended up without it? They obviously could not ride it any more. It was not forged of iron.

Lan Lan yelled at it again. The camel only groaned pitifully. 'You go on without me, I can't go any further,' it seemed to be saying. Ling Guan always said that camels would use every ounce of their strength to do what they had to do. They would drive themselves, literally, until they dropped. Maybe the bones had given it too much of a shock, thought Ying, the way someone with a terminal illness might be broken by the death of a comrade and give up the struggle too. Ying patted the camel. 'Don't be afraid!' she told it. 'You're not the same as those old bones.' But the camel only groaned, as if to say 'I'm not afraid, I just can't go on.'

The camel's hump was an empty bag of skin and its ribs stuck out. It was panting and from time to time stuck out its tongue. Its tongue was covered in thick brown and black calluses. It was obviously weak from lack of food, but it seemed to have had a collapse of morale too. Ying had no idea how to encourage it. She did not speak the camel's language and did not know what was going on in its head. But she was determined they should not abandon it, not only because a camel was worth two or three thousand yuan, but also because the beast was one of them now.

She suddenly realised why this place was littered with camel bones. The bones were such a reminder to passing camels that they, too, were going to die, that they had scared the live ones to death. When Han Tou was terminally ill, she remembered, he had fantasies of recovering. His life hung by a thread by then, but he clung on. When he finally realised what was in store for him, he died immediately. Their camel seemed to be in the depths of despair because so many other camels had died here. Even though camels had almost unlimited reserves of strength, the sight of so many bones had broken this one's resolve. She would never go the same way, Ying thought. Just so long as you felt alive, you would not die.

How could she save this animal that had given up all hope? She could not get inside its head, so she had to find some other way. In the end, the only idea she could come up with was to give the camel some of the cooking oil. Lan Lan frowned. 'This is the last we've got,' she said. 'Who knows how far we've got to go?' 'But we can't abandon our camel here,' said Ying. 'It came back for us of its own accord.' Lan Lan gave in. 'Fine, at least we'll die together.' 'Or live together,' said Ying.

Lan Lan got the bottle of oil out and gave it a shake. The oil coated the sides of the bottle in intricate swirls. Ying was heavy-hearted, and so, it seemed, was Lan Lan. There was just enough oil left for them to have two or three mouthfuls each. It was not much, but it was the last food they had.

The camel stared greedily at the liquid, just as it had done when they drank the oil previously. It obviously knew that the oil would taste good. Its masters had sometimes given it a lump of fat as a reward in the past. The oil had to be a lot better than dried stalks. The stalks staved off hunger but only if you could get them down, and the camel's tongue was as parched dry as the soles of hemp shoes and its gullet felt like sandpaper. This liquid was different, refreshing, smooth... Up till now, the camel could only watch greedily as the women swallowed this nectar. It could almost hear the glug-glug in their gullets, as dust-dry cells greeted the oil with a cry joyous as a thirsty sheep bleating on its way to the well. But up now, the camel could only look. Looking was all right. It had looked so much at the desert it was used to it. But the sight of the swirl of oil coating the sides of the bottle was almost too much to bear.

The camel never imagined that this lovely woman would give it oil to drink. She must be teasing. The villagers often teased camels. People said that hanging bunches of lucerne in their courtyards made donkeys love-sick. They played the same kind of tricks on camels too. The village kids thought it was a hilarious joke to hold out fresh grass, then snatch the grass away when the camel was near enough to take a bite. That was humans all over. In the past, the camel closed its eyes disdainfully when it was teased like this. But this oil was so very tempting. It was a pleasure just to look at it. There was pain in the pleasure, to be sure, rather like the tormenting excitement suffered by a young man watching a porn film, panting and red-faced but unable to tear his eyes from the screen.

The camel was the same.

Strangely, the bottle was actually being held to its muzzle. The camel knew how precious the bottle was to the women. It looked into the woman's eyes, as if to divine whether she was really teasing or not. But the eyes, to its surprise, were full of concern. The kind of concern it had seen in its mother's eye as a baby, when it caught its foot in a rat burrow and broke its leg. It would never forget a look like that. Don't underestimate a camel's memory. These animals can remember the face of a teasing human for a dozen years afterwards, just as it remembers that seven or eight years ago, someone gave it fresh grass to eat. Camels have one of the longest memories of all animals, even more so than horses. It is commonly accepted that camels, like horses, understand human nature, and that they are kinder-natured than horses too.

The camel was truly moved. It knew just what the look in this woman's eyes meant. She really was offering it a drink. It did not know that this was all they had left, but it knew just how precious the oil was. They had been taking a sip only once every couple of hours. When they drank, they closed their eyes and savoured the taste, as if imprinting the flavour on their very souls.

You drink it! The camel wanted to tell them. It had learned politeness from its master. When its master, who loved his booze, was offered a drink by someone else, he always said that. Of course, his master was just being polite, but the camel really meant it. However, it was impossible to make these humans understand, and that could not be helped. Besides, the camel knew that it was almost impossible to change a human's mind. It could not bear to deprive the women of this good oil. It would have been perfectly satisfied with a bowl of muddy water, even one with insects, bits of dead grass or tadpoles floating in it. But its mistresses could not drink dirty water, and they had so little oil left. The camel was determined to shake its head.

However, to its surprise, the woman forced its mouth open and pushed the bottle in. The liquid slid over its tongue. Its taste buds sprang to life, and shrieked like cicadas in the midday sun. It felt the strange, unforgettably intense flavour in the very depths of its being. It was more than a taste, it was a rush, a tsunami, of pure pleasure. The greedy craving of the buds on its tongue made it gape like koi carp waiting to be fed. With its tongue moistened again, it felt it could eat some of the dried grass, and once it had grazed, it would be able to carry these two lovely women again. It did not have any idea of human criteria for beauty, but it could see they were lovely in the eyes of human males. It had seen the way those two herders eyed them up earlier in the journey. They had stripped the women naked with their eyes.

The wondrously silky oil continued to trickle into its mouth, and slide soothingly down its throat. It swallowed, its gullet making a joyous wriggle like the movement of its penis when it mated with a female camel. Its throat was so dry that it could actually hear a rasping sound, the kind a snake makes as it sloughs its skin. Its throat was so cracked from dryness, it must look like the crazing on a dried-up river bed, it thought. That was why eating the dried grass made it feel as if its throat was being flayed. A throat should be slippery from a covering of mucous membrane, not parched like a dried-up river bed. A dry throat felt terrible, worse than Huo Bi Liang, a vicious bull camel in the village that invariably cornered all the female camels when they came on heat. When it caught them, it bit their hind legs and, no matter how hard the females tried to get away, the male had the leg in its mouth and it hurt too much to struggle free. Finally the female would submit, allowing the male to mount and mate with it. The female clearly did not enjoy Huo Bi Liang thrusting inside it. It looked away and uttered plaintive cries. Some of the females, however, stuck to Huo Bi Liang like glue after he had taken them by force a couple of times. Our camel was disgusted by such behaviour. But thirst was much worse than Huo Bi Liang. Thirst was invincible, and the proof was that it could conquer even Huo Bi Liang.

The camel felt the movement of its gullet and was happy. There was nothing more pleasurable than the sensation of oil slipping down a gullet as dry and cracked as the skin of a yam. It gave a groan like the involuntary moan the first time it had thrust into a virgin female camel. Bull camels liked to be the first inside a female, just like men did. But this oil was better even than mating with a virgin camel. The squirming and groaning of its gullet proved that, without a shadow of a doubt. You may never have heard the soft moan of a parched gullet taking in liquid-it is a true sound of nature, and music to the camel's ears. Imagine the burning sky above, and the burning heat all around, and then imagine the cooling oil permeating the depths of the camel's being. The camel felt immense gratitude to the woman who had given this gift. If I were a man, it thought, I would chase her. But it let the thought go. Dreaming was a bad habit, its nature told it that.

The oil reached its stomach, which greeted it with a joyful squirming. A camel's stomach was a monstrous thing. It started life dark red, then turned black and hardened until it had the texture of a half-cured piece of leather. It had shrunk in the hardening, and was as wrinkled as the face of an eighty-year-old woman, or the bark of a thorn bush on the sand dunes, or a pig's bladder hung under the eaves to dry in the sun for three days, or human afterbirth stewed for a whole day in soy sauce. This stomach made strange rasping sounds like three hundred mice all grinding their teeth in unison. At the same time, the stomach filled with grit. These were normally hidden in its crevices and folds, but now that the gastric juices had all gone, they emerged to flex their muscles and greet the oil that slid down from the gullet. The stomach was dark-opening its windows was the dholes' speciality-the grit could not see this cloudy liquid that came slithering in. The cells that lined the gullet along the way looted their share, but the smell of the oil, the vanguard, rushed up their noses. Do not underestimate the stomach. It is not just a bag of skin, it contains a whole world. Of course that world dies when you kill the animal and make the stomach into sausages, and all that's left is something stiff as a board. Just like the brain, in fact, full of plans and passions and tenderness when it's alive but, as soon as it arrives, dead, in your mouth, it is just another taste sensation-a bit gamey, a bit tasty. And you will never know all the stories it could once have told. They are gone forever. Well, the stomach is no different from that.

The sound of a squirming stomach is frightful. No words can

do it justice, in fact. Imagine yourself in the desert without water for three days, and your last breath is about to leave your body. Then imagine coming to a lake of fresh water. That's the noise you would make, and it comes not from the vocal chords, but the soul. It is like the howling of a tornado, filling the heavens, transformed into dancing, fighting hands. It's hard to put these down as musical notes. The camel did not like these thieving hands, they wanted to take possession of the oil. With shouts of Charge! and Kill!, they clattered past. Those sounds were embarrassing and the camel looked at the woman proffering the bottle in mute apology.

The bandit hands robbed the stomach of all this slippery liquid, mopping it up like a sponge, like a whale slurping up krill, until quite suddenly, there was not a single drop left. Expectantly these robbers waited for more. So did the camel. The woman shook the bottle to encourage the last drops from the inside of the bottle, and the camel felt the knocking against its teeth.

The woman threw the empty bottle into the gully. The camel wanted to tell her not to throw the bottle away. They could still re-fill it if they met herders or camel-drivers and could beg some water off them. It snorted. Of course the woman did not understand. Perhaps, it thought, she didn't like the idea of drinking from a bottle that had been in the mouth of a camel.

The camel looked sadly towards the gully. There was no help

for it. It was hers to throw away, nothing to do with the camel.

Then it saw the other woman retrieve the bottle, wipe the mouth of the bottle on her jacket and put it back in the bag that hung from its back.

21

The two women and the camel walked into the twilight. The camel was on its feet again, but could not carry them. Things were going from bad to worse. Riding a camel was not a comfortable experience—you got a sore bottom and terrible backache—but at least it was better than walking. Still, they had had some oil and, although it had not slaked their thirst, it had given them a bit of energy. They would need it for the steep climb ahead. They were not used to walking in sand, and their body fat had not turned into the sort of muscles you needed for trekking. Ying's calves stabbed with pain. With every step, the pain was excruciating. It was the same with the soles of her feet, they screamed until her whole body was limp with pain.

She tried to comfort herself by thinking that every step brought them closer to their goal, but they could see nothing but dark mountains all around them. Stars still hung low in the sky, but the women had lost interest in stars. They no longer saw the poetic flavour in them, as they had when they first got to the fine-sands. Poetic flavour was a luxury, she finally realised. A luxury they could only afford when they had enough to eat and drink and were not in any danger. They didn't even feel like singing the Gansu Hua'er songs. Ying understood now why so many women did not share her passion for Hua'er songs. They were too poetic when you were in a struggle for survival. Poetic flavour needed a degree of suffering, but when a great mountain of suffering weighed down on you, there was no room for poetic flavour.

They had better move on.

Looking at the indistinct track that stretched away in the gloom, she put poetry on hold, hardened her resolve and focused on hope. She hung on to the camel's tail, but didn't use it to pull her along except when they were going uphill. On the flat, she plodded along under her own steam, on leaden legs, so as not to be a burden on the camel.

Lan Lan had the camel's halter in her hand. She meant it to look as if she was urging it along, but really she was hanging on to it for support. Dad had given them the halter when they got to the fine-sands. The camel did not need it, because the rope was tied to the camels' nose-plug. But if you hung onto that, it would hurt the camel. A camel's nose was extremely sensitive to pain. The best way to get a disobedient camel to obey was to give the rope a shake, so that the beast got a sharp tug on its nose-plug. Then its eyes watered with pain. You want to see that? Try giving a camel a slap on its nose. The second way to bring a camel into line was to lash its nose with the whip. After a couple of lashes, the naughtiest camel would submit to being good. The halter was made of leather thongs knotted together, which fitted over the animal's head, so Lan Lan could safely hang onto it without hurting the camel's nose.

Ying hung onto the tail as she plodded through the sand, but she tried not to pull too hard. At least it was better for the camel than riding it.

Ying sometimes shut her eyes and drowsed, in spite of the pain in her legs. She had an overwhelming desire for sleep, and the only thing that kept her awake was when she tripped in the sand. Her need to sleep washed over her like the smell of fermenting liquor. Once she even let go of the tail and fell to the sand fast asleep, just as if she was in her own bed. Lan Lan turned to look back just at the moment that she turned the corner of a crescent dune and went back to pick her up. 'Lucky there was no wind,' she commented, 'or I would never have found you.' The wind not only covered all tracks, it would have carried away the sound of Lan Lan's calls. The wind made strange whistling noises, and would have lured Ying to a place where Lan Lan would never have found her. The wind had caused so many people to fall asleep and die in the sands.

Lan Lan decided to knot one end of a piece of rope around Ying's waist and the other end to the saddle. She made it long enough so that it was slack if Ying was hanging onto the camel's tail. She kept her hand on the rope so that if Ying fell asleep and the rope tightened, Lan Lan would know straightaway. It all depended, of course, on the camel behaving itself. If it shied at anything, it would jerk on the rope and pull Ying over. That would be as dangerous as falling off a horse and being dragged because your foot was stuck in the stirrup. To be sure that could not happen, Lan Lan made a slipknot in the end of the rope attached to the saddle pack. That way, she could simply pull it undone if she needed to.

The sisters-in-law stumbled along, half asleep. At the start of their journey into the fine-sands, the camel had a bell, but it got lost in the confrontation with the dholes. The only sounds as they walked along were the scuffing of their feet in the sand, and the occasional snort from the camel. This was explosive enough to make Ying jerk awake.

Their torch battery was rapidly running low, even though they were being sparing with it and only turned it on to see the way. Once, the torch-beam lit up the sinister shape of a skeleton. They might have shouted in surprise before, but they were used to such sights by now. In fact, if the skeletons were too far apart, Lan Lan worried that they had strayed off the track. Not all the bones were from camels, some were from dogs or perhaps foxes, they could not be sure. They had always heard that the shifting sands buried bones but, oddly, here it had not buried them, perhaps because the track was in the lee of the north-facing slope. That was only a conjecture though. There was a lot they did not know about nature. Not everything got buried in the sands, for instance Crescent Moon Springs in Dunhuang, which had remained exposed for hundreds, if not thousands, of years.

When it got to midnight, they could not walk any further. They stopped for a rest and Ying immediately fell asleep. Lan Lan was worried that she would fall asleep too, so she stayed on her feet. She knew they had to cover a certain distance by night. They were terribly thirsty. A little water remained in the plastic flagon, enough for a couple of sips each but, even though their throats were parched and burned, they did not dare touch it. Those few drops of water could save their lives, thought Lan Lan. If either of them fainted in the heat of the sun, at least the other could revive them with the water. Even such a small amount could postpone impending death.

The need for sleep was as irresistible as the approach of night, and death itself. Lan Lan got on the camel's back and dozed. She didn't make the camel lie down because if she had done, so she would have been in the land of dreams straightaway. Well, not dreams, she no longer had the strength to dream. So she sat on the camel's back as it stood. If it moved at all, she would surely wake up, she thought.

Then she shut her eyes. She felt as if she was falling into a great black void.

22

When Ying woke up, Lan Lan was still sound asleep. The camel had lain down to sleep and Lan Lan was propped up against it. Camels normally slept on their sides, with their legs extended, and experienced camel drivers never slept near their beasts in case they got crushed if the animal changed its position. But this one had been careful to go to sleep kneeling so that it posed no danger to its mistress.

It was fully daylight and Ying could see all around. Nearby lay a human skull, its teeth grinning at her, but Ying ignored it. She wanted to let Lan Lan sleep longer, but decided it would be better to move on while it was still cool. She had to prod her a few times to wake her up. Lan Lan opened her eyes wide in astonishment, as if she could not believe it was light already. 'How come I was so fast asleep?' she asked. 'Sometimes the body doesn't do what you want it to,' said Ying.

When they were less sleepy, they felt the onslaught of hunger and thirst, although hunger took second place to their overwhelming need for water. They had decided to hang on to the last few drops, but now they were so thirsty that Lan Lan changed her mind. She poured a little water into the lid of the plastic flagon and gave it to Ying, then poured some more for herself. They moistened their lips with their tongues, but it had no effect. Their lips had dried up like the skin of a yam and no amount of licking had any effect. Lan Lan's lips were swollen too, which was odd. How could she be so dehydrated and still have swollen lips?

They urged the camel to its feet and set off. Their bodies played tricks on them: If you kept going, it didn't hurt, or rather, you got used to it. If you took a rest, then started again, oh, how it hurt! For Ying, it felt much worse than the night before. They always said that the pain distracted you from your thirst, but no such luck: Ying found herself overwhelmed both by constant, stabbing pains and a terrible thirst. At least she was less sleepy, and walked along feeling more alert. She was not sure whether this was a good thing or not. She felt the physical discomforts more keenly too. She was so preoccupied that she paid no attention to where they were going, just focused all her attention on keeping going.

As they went on, the mountains turned to hills. There was very little vegetation, just the occasional withered stalk, which the camel ignored. They passed some camel dung. Lan Lan crumbled some between her fingers. It seemed very old. They passed a crescent dune with thorn bushes, its thorns covered in camel hairs. But the bushes were desiccated and dead, so any underground water must have dried up some time ago.

The visions of saltpans that filled Ying's head had begun to assume an overwhelming importance in her mind. She longed for them, the way she had longed for her lover. To both of them, Ying thought, the saltpans had come to represent the Buddhist Pure Land of Bliss, the only thing that could give meaning to their sufferings in this vale of tears.

Ying tried to distract herself by turning her mind to something different. She started with her lover. When he set out into the big wide world, had he faced the same terrible hardships, she wondered? She pictured Ling Guan's face covered in sweat, his lips swollen like Lan Lan's. He did actually look a little like Lan Lan. She was convinced that he must be suffering the same pain, the same hunger and thirst, the same despair…Everything that she was going through, he was going through too. She was comforted by the idea that they shared this suffering. She imagined herself telling him about their experiences, when they next met. They would be lying together on a secluded sandy hillside outside the village, her head pillowed on his chest, the desert breeze lifting her hair so that a few strands lay across his face. She closed her eyes, taking pleasure in telling him every detail of their thrilling desert journey. Of course, he would be startled, but not afraid for them. She felt his eyes on her, full of admiration and tenderness and, more than that, something that allowed her to draw his strength into the depths of her being. His heart would swell with emotion as he heard how these two frail women had confronted dholes as well as hunger, thirst, pain, despair and loneliness.

'Everything I've done, I've done for you,' she told him silently.

'He would gaze deep into her eyes when he heard this.' She conjured up the look in his eyes. This terrible journey, she thought, would become the proof of her love.

Then she turned her thoughts to the saltpans. She had no idea what they looked like, and perhaps for this reason, she imagined them as somehow mysterious, even totemic, as they struggled along in search of them. Of course, she hoped that getting to the saltpans would change her life. All her life, whenever the family's finances were tight, Lan Lan's dad would drive his camel to the saltpans. They represented hope. But what were they really like? She began to be anxious. If they did not live up to expectations when eventually, after so much hardship, they finally arrived, she would be heart-broken. She had had many hopes at different stages of her life. They floated in the air like so many soap bubbles, iridescent but evanescent. They burst and, with them, her illusions were shattered too, leaving her feeling desolate and empty. She hoped the saltpans would not be like this. She felt so exhausted, she could not put up with any more of these torments.

Stabbing pain and thirst woke her from her daydreams. The sun would soon hold sway again. The light kept getting into her eyes. These sandy slopes seemed to stretch into the distance, with no end in sight. Heavens know which fold of the sands the saltpan is tucked away in, she thought. She hardly dared raise her eyes to the horizon, because every time she did so, it filled her with despair.

They halted and had their last mouthful of water. They had not peed for two days. Every drop had been absorbed into their bodies. They were silent as they drank. They knew what this meant.

'Let's go,' said Lan Lan.

It was getting towards midday. Ying had imagined that they would go on resting by day and walking through the night, but their torch battery was exhausted and there was the danger that they would get lost in the dark. Besides, they were in such a bad way now that they consumed energy even when lying up in a deep hole. 'We might soon be there,' said Lan Lan. 'Might' was a word she was using a lot: They might meet someone, find a spring of fresh water, and so on and so forth. Every 'might' meant hope. So long as there was a 'might', they could get out of difficulty.

But midday got to them before the 'might' had materialized.

The sun would not stop blazing mercilessly down just because they were thirsty. Their bodies would not stop losing water just because of some future 'might'. The dehydration began through their heads, and they started to hallucinate and become disorientated. They did not mind the hallucinations, but the feelings of disorientation seemed to swallow them up. Lan Lan kept repeating that they must not let themselves fall asleep. Ying knew she was right. If they fell asleep, they would not wake up again. They kept encouraging each other to stay awake, even though their eyelids were stuck together by the dryness.

The first to collapse was the camel. Its nostrils flared and its eyes were half-closed. It panted as heavily as if a pair of bellows were working away inside it. Ying couldn't help thinking that it hadn't done too badly. Just that little bit of cooking oil had given it the energy to pull them up and over several mountains. But she was terrified when she saw it go down. Once it was down, they could do nothing for it. We're nearly at the saltpans, she urged it silently. Of course we are! We're nearly there, you can't collapse now. Lan Lan looked blankly at their camel and gave a long sigh.

The camel quivered and rolled onto its side, neck and legs stretched out. There were longer and longer intervals between each breath it took. If it died, they would have to pay the villagers back, but they weren't thinking of money now. Ying's main concern was that it should survive. It was the same concern that she had once felt for her husband as he hovered between life and death. But she was now so disorientated that all she could think was that the camel would soon be dead, and that she and Lan Lan would be next to go. She did not feel distressed, just unwilling to die.

Ying sat down. She did not mean to, but her legs gave way under her. So long as the camel was on its feet, they had support. But now it was down, and she knew she was incapable of getting over the next hill. Even if she did, what then? There were more hills in front. She was tired of thinking about them, all she wanted to do was to shut her eyes and sink into sleep. She knew that sleep would take her to the next world, but felt no concern about that. If your brain wanted to sleep, there was no help for it.

Lan Lan bit her lip. She looked at the camel, then at Ying. Her face was pinched and drawn, and streaked with sweat marks, and her nostrils were clogged with black dirt. Ying knew she must look just as bad, but she no longer cared.

'You hang on,' said Lan Lan, 'I'm going to look for water.'

Water? wondered Ying. But she knew it was better to go looking than not to look. If you looked, you might not find any, but staying here and not looking meant certain death.

Lan Lan didn't wait for an answer. She picked up the bottle and stumbled towards the gully to the north of them. She went very slowly. Her joints made a clicking sound and she looked like a walking skeleton. She might never come back, thought Ying.

Lan Lan made her way slowly around the hillock, leaving just emptiness behind. It was as if she was a drop of water that had been absorbed into the sand.

'Why have you left me all alone?' thought Ying. She felt aggrieved. If they were going to die, they should die together.

The camel was still panting heavily. Its eyes were closed and its diaphragm rose and fell. Ying wondered if there was a dhole inside, consuming its innards. The dholes were fearsome enough to squeeze into their bellies through someone's anus while they slept. The odd thing was that she did not feel fear. They could swallow them up for all she cared, first the camel, then her.

There was no sound to be heard in the gully. She remembered how the midday sun used to make a noise like the shrieking of cicadas, but now the sun was quiet. The camel's breathing gradually quietened. Although its diaphragm still heaved occasionally, it made no sound. She could no longer feel her heart beating. A great silence enveloped her. Had she already died, she wondered? She looked up at the sky. It was a woven blue cloth, and the clouds were silken threads. She wondered vaguely if they were running a race or trying to stay still…Then decided to stop thinking about them.

She still felt Lan Lan had done the dirty on her. She had not gone to look for water, she had abandoned her and gone to another world. A better world, of course. She had no sense of loyalty. If she wanted to go, she could have taken Ying with her. But she couldn't be bothered to complain. Her confusion was weaving a great net, which was about to be flung over her head. Spider's web or fishing net, it entangled her in its threads. She was convinced that it would ensnare her soul. She had never cared about her soul up till now. Her love for Ling Guan, she felt, was more physical than spiritual. Her soul had only re-surfaced when he had gone. But without the body, the soul could only suffer and pine. Let the net have her soul.

The camel lay on its side with all four legs stuck out straight, just as if it were asleep. It clearly had no energy left to kneel. Its blood must have gone claggy, like hers, in fact. The sun stuck out its tongue and threatened to lick away their last drops of moisture. Let it lick, it was big daddy, it could do what it wanted. There were no clouds in the sky, but Ying was so disorientated she did not feel hot, or even thirsty any more. Soon her soul would be immersed in confusion too. Fine, she thought, let it happen.

She wondered whether she should think about Ling Guan while she was still clear-headed, but the confusion already had her in its grip. It was so overwhelming, it was not surprising that she could no longer conjure up images in her mind. Memories of Ling Guan were painful, but it was a confused sort of pain. Her brain seemed very contrary. When she didn't want to see mental pictures of him, her brain seethed with them, setting her body and heart on fire. Now she wanted to think of him, she couldn't raise a flicker of a memory.

A black raven appeared on a hill not far away, croaking hoarsely. Ying knew she was going to die soon. Ravens loved human carrion, and their sense of smell was so acute they could even smell death on the living. They always cawed when someone was about to die, that was why they were regarded as 'birds of ill omen'. But Ling Guan told her that ravens were sacred, the creatures of the guardian bodhisattva, Gonpo. If they're sacred, I don't mind if I go to feed the ravens, Ying thought. She did not want to feed the dholes, but was content to feed the ravens. She just hoped that they did not start to feast on her body before her soul had left it. Apparently they always started with the eyes. She could not bear the thought of them pecking her eyes. How could they? She made up her mind that before she drew her last breath, she would turn on her belly and bury her face in the sand.

More ravens came, cawing loudly and staring at them. The camel opened its eyes, obviously aware what the strange noises meant. It looked at Ying and she looked back. In the glances they exchanged, there was mutual understanding, and helplessness. Her eyeballs suddenly felt scratchy, and there was a buzzing in her ears.

The bones they passed on their journey had probably been

stripped bare by those ravens, thought Ying. They must be looking forward to a meal of human flesh. There was nothing better, especially in the fine-sands. Apart from anything else, it was satiny smooth, nothing like the meat of other animals. Well, you can have me, she thought. Then another thought struck her: Had they come to her after eating Lan Lan's eyeballs? She had a vivid image of Lan Lan lying in the sands, her face covered in blood. Her brain was playing tricks on her again, not allowing her to see what she wanted to see and forcing bloody images on her which she did not want to see.

Ying shook her head violently.

Suddenly, the birds took off and circled overhead. How impatient they were! They must already regard her as dead, unless they were planning to peck at her while she was still alive, the way some humans liked eating the brains of live monkeys. Ying had no objection to them eating her when she was dead, but she drew the line at being eaten alive. She brandished the torch with its dead batteries at them, but discovered it was no good as a stick, so pulled off the whip which was tied to the camel's halter. The whip was a back-up. They brought it in case the camel became disobedient, to lash its nose. They had not used it because both camels were very well-behaved. As she whirled the thong in the air, she felt a black shadow loom over her. She lashed again, although really with no more energy, just a little faster. The raven obviously thought she was already dead, and was taken by surprise by the lash that suddenly came flying towards it out of nowhere.

There was a dull thud as the raven fell out of the sky into the gully.

The other birds squawked in fright and flew up to the top of the hill.

The bird on the sand fluttered and gave a few jerks, then lay still.

Ying thought she must be dreaming. She had never used the whip before, but she had mastered the trick of sending the thong flying through the air without wrapping it around her own body. The chance of hitting a bird was about as remote as a blind donkey finding grass, or a blind person getting a fried bun into their mouth. But with her first try, she had done it.

When she picked it up, she discovered it was just a fledgling, although it had looked like an adult bird on the wing. There were a few drops of blood in the sand. Its blood might keep her alive, thought Ying. She was by nature squeamish, but not any more. She seized the little corpse, thinking she would tear its head off and drink the blood. She failed to pull it off and, besides, the thought of covering her mouth with blood made her retch in disgust. The squirming in her belly made her suddenly clear-headed. Even if it meant she would die, she would not eat this filthy creature. She flung the bird away as hard as she could. It arched through the air a short distance, and rolled down into the gully.

When she got her breath back, she squinted at the birds in the distance. They looked back at her, as fearfully as she looked at them. Ying's dread was that they would peck out her eyes, and there would be nothing she could do to stop it. Why are you in such a hurry? she wanted to ask. You'll get me in the end anyway. She remembered she had said something like this to her brother-in-law, Meng Zi. That all seemed long, long ago. She wondered whether, if she had accepted him, he would have disgusted her too. She did not know.

Ying and the ravens faced off. The camel could see the drama but paid no attention. After everything that had happened, nothing could surprise it any more.

To Ying, she was a dead woman. It was going to happen sooner or later, she would become carrion for the ravens. She had not wanted to end up as food for the dholes, the night that they had had to fight them off, but that wasn't how she felt now. It makes no difference to me, she thought. She just didn't want to be eaten alive.

'It'll be soon,' she said to them. 'You won't have to wait long.' She felt her soul flitting away from her, as she slipped in and out of consciousness. When she lost consciousness completely, then her soul could go, she did not know where to, perhaps to Ling Guan.

She had heard that the soul of a dead person acquired magical powers and was able to see and hear anything it wanted, and appear in any place in an instant. But, just as she was afraid that the saltpans she longed to find might turn out to be a disappointment, she worried that Ling Guan might not live up to her expectations either.

What she was most afraid of was that just as her soul arrived at Ling Guan's door, he might be in there with the hairdresser girl. She was not sure why she had thought of the hairdresser and not any other girl, but that was her greatest fear. Her soul would be grief-stricken. Could souls weep tears? Perhaps not, but they could certainly make the sounds of sobbing. She knew that because village girls who hung themselves when they had been ill-treated, could be heard weeping in the darkness of the night. People had heard them. Would her soul do the same? She did not know. In life, she had never been much good at controlling her emotions, so how could she guarantee what she would do after death?

She would not think about Ling Guan, or whether he was mixed up with the hairdresser, or any other girl. She could not do anything about it, if that was the way he was.

She felt a chill in her heart. Fine, she thought, I knew what kind of a man you were when you were alive, I'm not going to turn into a weeping wailing ghost when I'm dead. She had obviously dreamed all this up, but now it had become reality. Feeling desolate, she wished the birds would come and start work now.

The birds cawed impatiently, but none of them dared risk the lash again. The camel was still panting like a bellows. As its mouth gaped, Ying could see its cracked and blackened tongue. It, too, was near death. We'll go together, she thought. Then she wouldn't be a lonely ghost. She had no hopes of Lan Lan. Lan Lan would end up in Vajravarahi's nirvana in the sky, her soul dispatched there by her final prayers. Ying would never catch her up. Ying was sceptical about Lan Lan's Buddhist heaven, and scepticim is the greatest enemy of self-cultivation. If she could not be with Lan Lan, then it was a good thing she had the camel's company, and that the camel didn't know how to get to nirvana. If the camel had been determined and believed it could achieve nirvana, then she, Ying, would be condemned to roam as a lonely ghost, because she could not bear to think of Ling Guan involved with that hairdresser.

Slow down, camel, don't go without me, Ying tried to say, but she could not get any sounds out. Her confusion had enveloped her in thick folds of netting. Her eyes, nose and mouth felt like they were clogged up by hairs floating in the air. The ravens had stopped cawing. They took off, flapping their wings noisily, and their wings turned into more netting. There were many nets now, and they enfolded her tightly.

Darkness fell around them.

23

She heard a faint, distant sound, a bit like her gran 'calling the soul' when she was little. Back then, if she started daydreaming, her gran would 'call her soul'.

She heard her gran's voice echoing from far away:

'Ying Ying! It's scary so far away, come closer!'

And someone answered: 'Coming!'

'Ying Ying! It's scary high up, come down!'

'Coming!'

'Ying Ying! It's hot up there, come and cool down!'

'Coming!'

'Ying Ying! That's a hungry place, come and eat!'

'Coming!'

'Ying Ying! Let all the spirits bring your body and soul together!'

'Coming!'

Her gran had plenty more calls like this. However far away she was, she would call her way to the kitchen, wrap a bowl full of noodles in a red cloth and press it to Ying's chest and back. After she'd done this for a few times, you could see a hollow in the middle of the noodles. 'See, that's what the soul was owed,' said gran, and topped up the noodles in the bowl. She would go on making her calls and pressing parts of Ying's body with the noodle bowl, until the noodles lay flat in the bowl, and the ritual was complete. That was what gran called 'calling up the soul'.

The answering voice she could hear was her mother's. Gran didn't ask her brother to answer for Ying because, instead of saying 'Coming!' when he was supposed to, he used to answer mischievously: 'I'm not coming!' That meant the magic wouldn't work and they had to wait for another propitious day and do the ritual again.

Gran's voice had a lingering sweetness like green rice soup, and her calls reached right into Ying's heart. When her gran died, there was no one to call up her soul for her any more.

As those long-drawn-out calls rang in her ears, she felt comforted. She must have already died. When your nearest and dearest departed, the only way to meet them again was to die yourself. She was glad she would get to see her gran again. Ying had always been her darling. When she was a little girl, her gran would cuddle her and call her 'my good little girl'. Gran was a mysterious old woman, rather like a shamaness, who always had crazy things like candies and peanuts squirrelled away in the folds of her clothing. She knew hundreds of ghost stories. Hearing them made Ying squeal with terror at night when the lights went out, and she always ran to her gran for comfort.

The calls Ying heard were like silk threads wrapping themselves around her and giving little tugs, as if she were a kite. The wind of life was insistently blowing her towards a bottomless abyss, but the silken threads were pulling her back again and, inch by inch, she allowed herself to be drawn closer and closer to the caller. The calls seemed to be changing. Now the voice sounded like Lan Lan.

Ying forced herself to open her eyes. Her eyeballs felt rough as sandpaper and it was a struggle, but finally the light shone into them. At first, she could see nothing but the glare.

'Quick! Eat these!' Lan Lan sounded jubilant.

Lan Lan was holding out a black stick to her. When Ying did not move, Lan Lan scraped the black skin off with the whip handle. Underneath the pith was pure white. Ying looked at it. She had eaten it before: The villagers stewed it with mutton, after they slaughtered the sheep at the beginning of winter. She remembered its name, cynomorium.

Lan Lan broke off a piece and pushed it into Ying's mouth. Ying nibbled it and a sweet liquid flooded her mouth. Ying had only ever seen this herb dried, and was surprised that the fresh stalk contained so much juice.

Lan Lan fed Ying with more of the cynomorium stalk, then unfolded the towel she was wearing around her head. Ying was amazed to see that the towel was full of cynomorium.

Lan Lan chewed another bit and fed it to the camel. The animal was panting heavily, but stretched out its blackened tongue with a tremendous effort and swallowed the juice that Lan Lan put into its mouth.

The cynomorium was the most delicious thing Ying had ever eaten. The juice trickled between her teeth and over the taste buds on her tongue. Greedily, the taste buds clamoured for more, gaping like hungry sparrow nestlings when the parent bird arrives back at the nest with a worm. The sweetness aroused long-forgotten sensations in her belly, which began to rumble frantically.

The camel started on its own piece, chomping noisily, and dribbling juice from the corner of its mouth. Lan Lan was jubilant. 'Eat this one,' she told Ying. 'After we've had a rest, I'll go and dig some more. There are plenty in that gully.'

Lan Lan tried to get the camel to its feet. It struggled and stumbled and finally stood, unsteadily. The cynomorium had slaked its thirst, and satisfied its hunger. Its soul had returned to its body. Ying had a headache but was no longer disorientated. 'That's enough,' Lan Lan told her. 'No more for now.'

Leading the camel, they made their way to the gully. It was not far, just the other side of the sand-spit. There was soil mixed with sand underfoot. When Lan Lan found a fissure, she tapped her foot. It sounded hollow. 'That's where the cynomorium grow,' she said. 'Under here is full of them. The ones you've just eaten I dug out of a ditch.' Ying looked around. There were cracks all over the place, rather like the cracks when the yam burst through the soil. There were cynomorium just pushing their way through the surface. 'Heaven helps those who help themselves,' said Ying.

'It was Vajravarahi who saved us,' said Lan Lan. 'Believe me, I walked past the sand-spit into the gully and knelt down and prayed to her. I said, "Vajravarahi, if I get out of the fine-sands alive, I'll re-build your temple and have your statue gilded again." After a little while, I saw what I thought was herders, reddish shadows in the distance, and I rushed towards them. But what I found was the cynomorium. So when I get back, I'm going to raise the money and do what I promised. I can't fail her now, can I?' Lan Lan said very earnestly. Ying was sceptical. You might have just been seeing things, she wanted to say. But she said nothing. If it really was the Dorje Pakmo who had saved them, then it would be hurtful to cast doubt on it, not to mention blasphemous. 'Thank heavens for Vajravarahi,' was what she actually said.

Lan Lan hacked open the crack in the ground. Underneath, it was full of cynomorium. These are parasitic succulents with a single stalk around a foot long, reddish-black in colour, which grow in sandy soil and are famed for their restorative medicinal properties. The largest can grow to thirty or forty pounds in weight and crack the surface of the soil as they force their way through, so there is no need to dig for them. Lan Lan scraped the soil and sand from a root with the handle of the whip and threw it to the camel. The camel gave a loud, excited snort.

Lan Lan and Ying unsaddled the camel and dug a ditch for themselves on a north-facing slope. They ate again, tethered the camel, crawled into the ditch and fell asleep. They woke, ate, napped and ate again…They felt fortified by the rest and the sleep.

The next morning, Ying found some seashells. So the desert must once have been covered in a great sea, she thought. If even an ocean could turn into a desert, how much more vulnerable were humans…In no time at all, she would be old, and Ling Guan too. What was the point in him going to seek a better future, since we were both going to get old? She felt resentful.

She put away these thoughts from her mind and dug up more cynomorium. She would load up the camel with cynomorium and carry on going her own way.

24

Finally, a glittering whiteness met their eyes.

It dazzled against the yellow, sun-drenched sands. It was only when they drew closer that they realised the earth was encrusted with salt. Here, there was not a blade of grass to be seen. The combination of blazing sun and saline water underground had baked the earth spongy soft like a steamed bun. The air was moister than before, and smelled of the sea.

Lan Lan was happy. 'We're nearly at the saltpans,' she said. 'This is what the edge is like.'

The camel snorted triumphantly.

Ying, who should have been excited, felt an odd sort of tranquillity instead.

She was afraid that this thing she had longed to find would, once again, prove unknowably strange.

图书在版编目（CIP）数据

雪漠小说精选 = Selected Stories by Xuemo：英文 / 雪漠著；（英）韩斌（Nicky Harman）译. —北京：中国大百科全书出版社，2018.5

ISBN 978-7-5202-0278-7

Ⅰ. ①雪… Ⅱ. ①雪… ②韩… Ⅲ. ①短篇小说-小说集-中国-当代-英文 Ⅳ. ①I247.7

中国版本图书馆CIP数据核字（2018）第096691号

出 版 人　刘国辉

特约编审　阿去克

策划编辑　李默耘

责任编辑　姚常龄

特约编辑　刘 彦　王人龙

英文校对　石学亮

责任印制　邹景峰

封面设计　U-BOOK

出版发行　中国大百科全书出版社

地　　址　北京阜成门北大街 17 号

邮　　编　100037

网　　址　http://www.ecph.com.cn

电　　话　010-88390739

印　　刷　北京市十月印刷有限公司

开　　本　880 毫米 ×1230 毫米　1/32

字　　数　86 千字

印　　张　8.125

版　　次　2018 年 5 月第 1 版第 1 次印刷

定　　价　58.00 元

本书如有印装质量问题，请与出版社联系调换